T0149260

MONDAY
Morning
MOMENTS

MONDAY Morning MOMENTS

JUNE JONES

MONDAY MORNING MOMENTS

iUniverse books may be ordered through booksellers or by contacting:

iUniverse
1663 Liberty Drive
Bloomington, IN 47403
www.iuniverse.com
1-800-Authors (1-800-288-4677)

ISBN: 978-1-5320-1677-6 (sc)
ISBN: 978-1-5320-1678-3 (e)

Library of Congress Control Number: 2017902123

Print information available on the last page.

iUniverse rev. date: 02/14/2017

DEDICATION

I would like to dedicate this book with the vision, wisdom, and insight, along with the perseverance given to me to write, to all the readers, hearers, and doers of the word. Above all, I thank God for His precious, benevolent love and for giving me the awesome gift of conveying words to help, comfort, encourage, uplift, inspire, and redirect and influence attitudes in others.

In addition, I am grateful to bestow my deep affection and appreciation to my high school sweetheart and husband, Andrew, for his unwavering support, love, patience, and encouragement while I wrote my thoughts and compiled them into a noteworthy vehicle to be read and distributed. Also thanks to my daughters, Allison and Suzette, and to my granddaughters, Joy, Rachel, and Keziah, all in college out of state, for their words of praise and encouragement.

Many thanks to my Red Hat Society "Corona Jewels" sisters, my Praise Tabernacle Bible Church family, and my many relatives and friends. I would like to thank all the recipients of *Monday-Morning Moments* who said that what I wrote about on a particular Monday morning was exactly what they needed to read, that it was a great way to start the week, or that it was something they'd been going through the past week ("And how did I know that?"). I am privileged to share the joy of writing by being the conduit through whom the Word is processed, shared, enjoyed, and implemented in someone's everyday life after reading *Monday-Morning Moments*. Writing has become an outlet for the creation of my ministry, 'making a difference and sowing seeds for change'.

ACKNOWLEDGMENTS

June was exposed to church, preaching the Word and gospel music by way of her mother and grandmother. Jesus had full control of her life early in her marriage, when she started working in 1965 as a general-duty nurse at Receiving Hospital, which was a city hospital in Detroit, Michigan. After leaving Receiving, she was hired in 1970 at Northwest General Hospital and then retired from the field in 1984. June went back to school at the Control Data Institute in Southfield, Michigan, to learn computers, and upon graduation she was hired as a service technician at Xerox Corporation, ultimately retiring as a senior customer service engineer in 1998. June relocated from Southfield, Michigan to Chino Hills, California, Her quest to intimately know God ultimately led her to Life Bible College in San Dimas, California, where she graduated magna cum laude with a BA in Biblical Studies and a minor in Pastoral Ministry in 2008.

In response to the Lord's question when He asked Isaiah, "Whom shall I send and who will go for us?" Isaiah said, "Here am I, send me Lord" (Isa.6:8 NIV). June began her ministry, Making a Difference, Sowing Seeds for Change, with the sole purpose of affecting a lasting transformation in someone's life through the Word, constant prayer, and an intimate relationship with God. It has been an honor and a privilege to have written, and continue to write, Monday-morning words of encouragement, inspiring people to make a difference and sow seeds for change. I would like to especially thank the iUniverse team for their encouraging words to write, revise, proofread, edit, and write some more until my publication was satisfactory and paramount for a job well done!

INTRODUCTION

I found out that writing a book is a fairly easy task, but it is not the same as having to write, and then have your work printed for others to read, because there is a publishing process that definitely has to be followed. That being said, I would like to thank God for giving me wisdom, insight, and perseverance and for His love and the precious gift of conveying words to help, encourage, comfort, uplift, and inspire others by being the conduit through whom He speaks.

Writing early every Monday morning is a fantastic way for me to reach out to others, as well as share my Holy Spirit inspired words of wisdom and encouragement. Teaching and writing are my passion, and writing early on Monday morning prioritizes my daily activities and frees my mind from doubt and worry. When I write my story, it will survive me, as I am able to tell it. Also, it is good for me to write about the blessings bestowed upon me, as well as the missteps of life and let people know how I survived through specific experiences.

Write simply to tell someone you love or miss them. Write about what you have done for others and their response to you. Write to remember the good and work on the bad. Write to take a stand against oppression. Write for no reason at all, except to exercise your brain and other parts of your body. Keep a pad handy to write down pertinent life events, and sometimes write just for the sake of it!

ABUNDANT BENEFITS

When you begin to analyze and summarize all the benefits you have been so freely given, you probably realize you didn't used to think twice about them. We possess the benefits of sight, speech, hearing, smell, and touch. We have the ability walk, talk, breathe, and laugh. Most notably, we have the benefit of being able to openly worship and read the Word. We also have the benefit of the sun, which warms the earth, makes things grow, provides us with energy and daylight, and gives us the essential vitamins A and D. "Blessed of the Lord be his land, for the precious things of heaven, for the dew, and for the deep that lies beneath, and for the precious fruits brought forth by the sun, and for the precious things put forth by the moon" (Deut. 33:13–14 KJV). Also, we benevolently have the Son of God, who radiates in our spirit, allows all the components of the fruit of the Spirit to grow within us and gives us the assurance of victory, and most precious of all gives us eternal life.

As you mercifully accept and appreciate all the abundant gifts freely given to you, be blessed with all the lifetime benefits you have acquired. However, don't hesitate to tell others how they too can obtain the same amazing benefit package free of charge for life, and simply by asking.

ACCOUNTABILITY

Ponder for a moment the issue of accountability. Being liable or answerable comes into play when an imminent situation comes up unexpectedly and has to be dealt immediately, decently, and in order. Accountability should be present in a lot of areas in our lives: our homes, marriages, churches, schools, neighbors, and especially our jobs. Accountability is doing the best, honest, responsible, and most answerable obligation or task you have to perform. Whatever your status in life may be—your age, culture, occupation, duty, or responsibility—accountability should always be foremost in your life.

It is the standard by which we operate at our highest level of humanity, taking responsibility of what we are purposed and called to do. It is the testing of our own actions and living with integrity, courage, honesty, and faith. "And let us not grow weary while doing good, for in due season we shall reap if we do not lose heart. Therefore, as we have opportunity, let us do good to all, especially to those who are of the household of faith" (Gal. 6:9–10 NKJV). Remember—accountability is priceless.

ADVERSITY IS A GIFT

Adversity is an unfortunate event or misfortune, a negative circumstance, a condition of distress, or possibly a calamity. However, a gift is something that is given freely or voluntarily, without payment expected or required. Adversities may come to us, whether invited or not: an accident that totaled your car, your doctor's diagnosis that was not favorable, and the teacher who sent your youngster to the office for disrupting the class for the third time. The bank notified you that your charge cards had been comprised, the power went off, and all the food in your refrigerator is beginning to smell. All of these adversities cannot hardly be gifts, so don't hold too tightly to them, trying to figure them out.

However, adversity will resonate within and cause you to stand when you want to sit down, stay and face the problem when you want to flee, develop stamina when you want to quit, persevere when everything is going wrong, and go back when you need to go forward. "My brethren, count it all joy, when you fall into various trials, knowing that the testing of your faith produces patience" (James 1:2–3 NKJV). Ultimately, adversity is a gift that will resonate in the new victorious you, for everything you have been called and purposed to do.

A Healthy Heart

Get to know your healthy heart, because it is the place where the life blood of your body flows out of, the place where Jesus was invited to come in and live, and the place where His Word is hidden that you might not sin against Him (Ps. 119:11). A healthy heart abundance allows the mouth to speak of love, truth, and righteousness. However, unforgiveness sometimes overshadows love and the goodness of God, and all the elements around you are jaded, dimmed, and meaningless. Forgiveness is a necessary element directed toward healing, wholeness, restoration, and empowerment. It justifies you, purifies your heart, and removes mountains of guilt from your life. Freedom from depression enables you to stand up to worldly assaults that are easily overcome with a healthy heart filled with God's love.

Remember that God is love and that "we love Him because he first loved us" (1 John 4:19 NKJV). Enjoy your blessings as you venture out into a dark world and, from a healthy heart, spread the fruit of the Spirit, which that consists of joy, peace, patience, kindness, goodness, gentleness, faithfulness, self-control—all of which are securely wrapped up in merciful love. Let your healthy heart beat to the rhythm of life with rejoicing love.

All in a Day's Journey

Running a marathon is no easy task—not exactly your everyday activity or an "all in a day's journey" situation. It takes months of physical and mental training to get your body conditioned to run 26.2 miles. An ordinary journey is the act of traveling from one place to another, which usually starts with walking. Walking is an action verb; it requires movement that gets you moving with intent to some planned destination. Some folks walk for exercise to get fit and stay fit, and some people walk to stave off an illness. Perhaps some people walk because they don't own a car. Others walk because they might not have any bus fare, or there is no bus route where they live. One good thing about walking it doesn't require any special equipment, shoes, or clothes; it's free and can be fun as well as beneficial.

If it's too hard, boring, or time consuming, invite someone to journey on your walk with you. It might be a lifesaver that develops into friendship, fellowship, and love. "But many that are first shall be last; and last shall be first" (Matt. 19:30 KJV). Keep moving and putting one foot in front of the other, and your day's journey will be accomplished with purpose, pleasure, and peace.

AMAZING GRACE

We know the song "Amazing Grace" and its first verse: "How sweet the sound, that saved a wretch like me! I once was lost but now I'm found, was blind but now I see." But have you ever wondered about the sweet sound and just what it is? Perhaps it is the sound of when the specialist said all your diagnostic tests were negative, or another surgeon told a relative that her operation was successful. How sweet it is when the physician says you're pregnant after years of trying to conceive. Absolutely it's the sweet sound of your baby's first cry after birth. Perhaps it's the sound of screeching brakes to avoid someone who ran a stop sign. Maybe it's the sound of my neighbors' keys unlocking the front door of a home they thought they could never afford to own. It's the sound of the supermarket cash register totaling up the receipt for food after you prayed that God would stretch your money to the end of the month, and He did!

What sweet sounds in your life are related to "Amazing Grace"? After Paul asked God three times to have the thorn in his side removed, the Lord said, "My grace is sufficient for you, for my power is made perfect in weakness" (2 Cor. 12:9 NIV). Begin to reflect on all the "Amazing Grace" moments that have emerged in your lifetime, and remember the sweet sounds of life and who provided them.

ANYONE CAN TEACH

How can we change some of the negative habits and perceptions for children regarding teaching and learning? First of all, we can prepare and readily accept change so we can stretch beyond ourselves and willingly move to expand. When we validate a regular reading program, we can start by reading books, and we embrace change when we enroll in an educational course for advancement and improvement.

Second, we can exercise our gifts by reading our Bible and many other books for encouragement, development, and personal growth. We should pray for our children and the other students in various schools, both individually and as a group.

Third, find ways to be involved and assist students to channel their energies, but be careful not to squash their enthusiasm or their personalities. "Give instruction to a wise man, and he will be yet wiser; teach a just man, and he will increase in learning" (Prov. 9:9 KJV). Concentrate on making a difference as you sow seeds for change into people, and watch their transformation to become willing and receptive vessels. They just might become faithful, available, and teachable students who can emerge into thirsty students always wanting to learn. Remain on the lookout for teachable moments to inspire and expand their sphere of knowledge.

ARE YOU LISTENING?

Listening is an act of making a conscious effort to hear, pay attention, or take advice. Are you listening to the voices of your spouse, children, coworkers, or friends when you have conversations, offer advice, or have complaints about something happening in their lives? Listening is an art of actively engaging in what other people are saying to you and giving your undivided attention to their words. Perhaps you have realized that sometimes folks don't want your advice; they simply want you to listen to them. Oftentimes they need to hear themselves speak what is on their minds, maybe to audibly hear what they are thinking. Perhaps they need to know you are someone who will listen when the world has beaten them up, circumstances have turned out all wrong, and life seems not to be fair.

Are you listening when there are lessons that need to be learned, the Word needs to be spoken, or an error needs corrected? "For out of the abundance of the heart the mouth speaks" (Matt, 12:34b KJV). Consequently, take heed and watch how often you speak out of your abundant thoughts, whether good or bad. Note how often you actively listen to what people are saying, really listen to the world of wondrous sounds all around you, and observe the activities of life for all its richness with clarity.

Are You a Leader or a Follower?

Leadership involves being an effective leader who strives to include and educate others to implement improvements and bring about the needed changes. A good leader must accept responsibility to facilitate, cultivate, and overcome the resistance to change, with an attitude of forging ahead to make a difference. Followers must have a reason to assemble; often they will follow a person of trust, honesty, responsibility, and organization. If their positions and opinions are valued they will respond with a positive attitude and a great work ethic. "And if you have not been faithful in what is another man's, who will give you what is your own? (Luke 16:12 NKJV).

Both leaders and followers are needed to complete projects, set goals, and achieve final results. They interact well when they have integrity, develop good working relationships, have significant dialogue, show positive attitudes, listen to each other, and care about what happens to them. In reality, leaders and followers together make meaningful contributions to a team, an establishment, a home, a community, and your church. Ask yourself, "Am I a leader or a follower?" The answer is whatever is within your comfort level of expertise to do.

BEAUTY INSIDE AND OUTSIDE

For a special occasion, you might start to clean your house, dust the furniture, vacuum the carpet, and set out the best dishes and glasses. Long-forgotten distant relatives, family, and friends are coming to gather for food, fellowship, and friendship. Could the occasion be the birth of a child or grandchild, a wedding, a graduation, or a funeral? You've got to make sure that everyone looks nice, smells good, is on best behavior on the outside, and has a nice time with all the festivities.

But what about the inside—the issues hidden in your heart, your mind, your emotions, or your attitude? Perhaps it is anger, bitterness, frustration, and unforgiveness over something so trivial that you probably don't remember what it was anyway, and it really doesn't even matter anymore. "He has made everything beautiful in its own time" (Eccles. 3:11 NKJV). As you reflect on all the things you have to be thankful for, continuously pray for the ability to be more compassionate, giving, and forgiving. Exhibit your inner beauty while you strive to be more loving. Don't forget those less fortunate than you are; extend some of your abundant inside beauty and love to those on the outside, for all to see.

BEING ALONE

Being alone means experiencing peace and quiet, having solitude, or being without anything. But is that a bad or good thing? Certainly you will have time to think things through without any other input. Being alone affords you time to pray, sing out loud, visit someone who is sick, do some community service projects, or practice for an upcoming speaking engagement. It gives you time to do something for yourself: go to the library and catch up on your reading, browse in the mall, have a massage, get a pedicure or new hairdo, watch a movie, and cry out loud. Being alone lets you take the time to prioritize your schedule—or maybe just do nothing!

Know that being alone is not the same thing as being lonely, which is without a choice. "It is written, Man does not live by bread alone, but by every word that proceeds from the mouth of God" (Matt. 4:4 NKJV). Rejoice in the life choices you have and share your time, talent, and treasure with those who are lonely to brighten their world. Let them know that it is okay to be alone, but it's not okay to be lonely.

BE STILL AND KNOW

"Be still and know" is a simple phrase that means to behold the wonders of the universe, the sun by day and the moon and stars by night, the change of seasons at their appropriate time of trees and flowers blooming and then fading away. It includes the wonders of the human body: when to breathe, eat, sleep, digest, eliminate, multiply, grow up, and grow old. "For I know the thoughts that I think toward you, says the Lord, thoughts of peace, and not of evil, to give you a future and a hope" (Jer. 29:11 NKJV). Know that you are loved and set apart for greatness in the kingdom, to be a light that shines bright in dark places and to be salt that seasons and savors. Know you are loved and not cursed, up and not down, rich and not poor, healthy and not sick, sane and not suffering, happy and not sad, joyful and not sorrowful.

We have to be still so our minds can listen more clearly, and for our spirits to receive God's love poured out for us. Be still and know without a doubt about the life experiences that will lead you to nurture, mentor, and mature others along destiny's path. Joy will come from calm, peace, serenity, freedom, and your general well-being. "Be still and know" means having absolute love and happiness when you listen, laugh, and love in the stillness of life.

BEING A SERVANT AND
NOT A SLAVE

A servant is someone who gives of herself freely, with humility and a pleasant attitude or outlook on life, without expecting any reward or recognition. In other words, a servant gives because she wants to give out of the benevolence of her heart.

However, a *slave* gives because he has no other choice, except maybe anger, rejection, unmet expectations, and unfulfilled goals that keep him bound to negative habits and attitudes. Perhaps being a slave is blocking all the elements of the fruit of the Spirit from manifesting in his life, and that may cause him to look on the downside instead of the upside of his life.

Bridging from slave to servant will produce an atmosphere to responsively make a difference and sow seeds for change in people's lives as well as the lives of others. Look in the mirror and advocate for change from slave to servant; never again be bound by the cares, influences, and whims of the world. "Choose for yourselves this day whom you will serve, but for me and my house we will serve the Lord" (Josh. 24:15 NKJV). You can consciously seek ways to change your attitude and your outlook. A makeover will enlighten for all to see, learn, and absorb that you can go from a slave mentality to being a willing and loving servant who freely gives herself away to the world.

BROKENNESS

What does brokenness mean? Could it mean fractured, splintered, weakened, bankrupt, violated, or not in good working order? We are God's treasure in earthen vessels, and sometimes our vessels wobble a little bit or develop a fine-line crack; possibly our joy seeps out, our light grows dim, our walk slows down, and our anointing loses its power. Maybe all of these actions occur because of our disobedience, grieving the Holy Spirit through insensitivity, daily living distractions, ministry, and spiritual warfare.

But the potter is always ready, willing, and able to mend His earthen vessels. "But now, O Lord, thou art our Father; we are the clay, and thou our potter; and we all are the work of thy hand" (Isa. 64:8 KJV). Subsequently, we have to humbly go to Him in repentance and prayer, and with the regular reading of the Word. We must be steadfast with our praise and worship, and we should also remember that God dwells in the praises of His people.

Line yourself up to be blessed because you can have a spin on the potter's wheel to mend the brokenness of your earthen vessel, if it is necessary. Afterward, you'll be joyously mended and filled to overflowing with treasure, to be used for building up God's kingdom here on earth.

BE THANKFUL

Be thankful you do not have everything you desire, because if you did, you wouldn't have anything to look forward to. Be thankful when you don't know something; it gives you the opportunity to learn. Be thankful for the difficult times, because they will give you the opportunity to grow. Be thankful for your limitations, because they afford you an opportunity for improvement. Be thankful for each new challenge, because it will build up your strength and character. Be thankful for your mistakes, because they will teach you valuable lessons. Be thankful when you're tired and weary, because it means you worked to make a difference. "And let the peace of God rule in your hearts, to which also you are called in one body; and be thankful" (Col. 3:15 NKJV).

You may realize that it is easy to be thankful for the good things. However, a life of rich fulfillment comes to those who are thankful for the speed bumps in their life, which caused them to slow down, look around, and turn all their negatives into joyous, everlasting positives. Eventually, you may have an opportunity to look back on your life and be thankful to know that all your troubles can and will become your blessings.

BINDING BEHAVIORS

An inability to move forward in life might be due to binding behaviors, if something keeps coming up at an inappropriate time. Maybe things are never good enough, and so they often produce anger and hostility. Could be you have an expectation to have your everyday needs met in a certain manner, but you don't have the resources? A lack of funds could possibly lead you to start lying, stealing, and cheating to get what you want. Perhaps uncontrolled outbursts, mood swings, and discipline problems are traced to spiritual discontent and an ineffective prayer life. Low self-esteem from the lack of a positive environment and the fear of never having enough may cause you to turn away from God, who is the source for everything you need. All of these undesirable activities could stem from binding behaviors that ultimately will produce negativity in your life.

However, if you can identify the binding behaviors and own up to the responses they create in your life, then change for the better can come into your life permanently. "And do not be conformed to this world, but be transformed by the renewing of your mind, that you may prove what is that good and acceptable and perfect will of God" (Rom. 12:2 NKJV). Take some enthusiasm to cultivate a loving, forgiving, and peaceful frame of mind for a lifestyle change with great benefits for all.

BLESSED TO BE A BLESSING

The privilege that we have is a choice to choose, and it is truly a blessing because so much of the world lives in an environment of restraint from their government, financial institutions, religious affiliates, and cultural and historical customs. We are blessed to live in a country that allows freedom to live anywhere we choose, attend the church of our faith, send our children to a school of our choosing, drive any car we can afford, dress in clothes we like to wear, and attend entertainment venues we support.

However, with blessings come responsibility. Our obedience is tied to what we receive and how much we pass along to help others. "Blessed be the God and Father of our Lord Jesus Christ, who hath blessed us with all spiritual blessings in heavenly places in Christ" (Eph. 1:3 KJV). The blessed benefits we accrue are peace, joy, patience, kindness, goodness, faithfulness, gentleness, and self-control, and they are all wrapped in God's love. We are blessed when we are forgiven of our sin, redeemed from a life of jealously and pride, healed from all manner of sickness and diseases, protected from dangers seen and unseen, and have our wants and desires satisfied within reason.

You will be unconditionally blessed to be a blessing to someone, sometime, somewhere, and somehow in all you put your hand to do, in a world truly in need of blessed folks.

BUILDING BRIDGES

Building bridges will eventually connect all of the man-made barriers in your life. Initially, you might need to consider building bridges to cross over to healing and wholeness, or to obtain the peace that passes all understanding. Build bridges so that you can experience forgiveness that empties your heart to be filled with God's love. Bridges will release you from pain, anger, and bitterness that have a tight grip on your happiness, which will keep you from being victorious in your daily life activities. Think about building bridges so you can reconcile with a loved one or a friend who allowed a disagreement to sever a relationship about something that happened so long ago you don't even remember why. Attempt to strengthen the atmosphere in your home, community, and church.

This process requires honesty, trust, faith, and action on your part. "The discretion of a man makes him slow to anger, and his glory is to overlook a transgression" (Prov. 19:11 NKJV). Push yourself to be a person others know to be different, because God can use anyone at any time to fulfill His purpose for the kingdom. He also can use someone who is willing to build bridges over hate, misunderstanding, and despair, which seem to be so prevalent in the world today.

BUILDING OTHERS UP
IN THE FAITH

Faith building means to tell others about the goodness that has happened in your life and what God has done for you. Confidently ask others about their salvation and beliefs. Do they own a Bible? If they are receptive, then take some time to nurture them through the Word. Invite them to Bible study and encourage them to read and meditate on the Scripture daily. Maybe after a while, teach them about memory verse exercises and how to do them. Discuss various characters in the Bible, their circumstances, and how they overcame certain situations. Share biblical principles that are applicable to their lives. Give them the confidence to know the Word, read the Bible for themselves, and realize they were once sinners but now they have eternal salvation. "For all have sinned and fall short of the glory of God" (Rom. 3:23 NKJV).

If each person could seek one, reach one, teach one, and save one, then we would be much closer to our eternal reward, which is the return of Jesus Christ. However, you must be diligent to seek those who desperately need building up in the faith for the good of everyone to continually pass on and share with others.

BREAKING YOKES

A yoke is a device used to harness a pair of animals together for increased plowing or pulling, such as a wagon. It also is a mark or symbol of oppression, slavery, or servitude—something that binds, unites, or connects. A yoke can be a positive or a negative asset, however it is used.

The act of breaking yokes means that something has bound you, enslaved you, or captured your environment, and it needs to be dealt with and eliminated. Perhaps it's breaking the yokes of credit card debt with overspending and endless bills. Break the yoke of eating too much unwholesome food with an unannounced weight gain, or without enough exercise. Could it be too much TV, Internet, and texting and not enough reading, praying, and family time? "Take my yoke upon you and learn from me, for I am gentle and lowly in heart, and you will find rest for your souls. For my yoke is easy and my burden is light" (Matt. 11:29–30 NKJV).

Yoke breaking in your life will eventually lift you out of the mediocrity and poverty way of life and into an atmosphere of unspeakable joy, peace, and restoration. As you twist, cut, chop, wiggle, and break out of the yokes, it will allow you to be enveloped and will nurture you into a marvelous new lifestyle and a never-before-experienced way of doing things.

CARRYING A BURDEN

When you are carrying a burden, it can be worrisome. Perhaps it's a heavy workload, an unwanted assignment, or a duty that is boring or unpleasant. Sometimes it's hard to focus on life when you're bogged down with the weight of situations and see no solution or conclusion in sight. When you are carrying a burden of bitterness, anger, jealousy, rage, or low esteem, it is hard to make good decisions, have energy, and have enough focus to have a productive day.

Are you carrying someone else's burden? Who will benefit from your carrying a burden, anyway? Will your quality of life improve? When you empty yourself and detach yourself from carrying a burden, then the fruit of the Spirit will bloom in the garden of your heart, with new possibilities and increased confidence that will manifest in your life. Unload the trunk of your car, desk drawers, the kitchen pantry, and the garage of stuff to avoid carrying a burden. Eliminate the pressure of being bogged down with unhealthy relationships and any other activity that weighs you down. Avoid losing focus on what is important in life, which is life itself, filled with a relationship with the One who "created the heavens and the earth" (Gen. 1:1).

CELEBRATE AND REMEMBER

Remember and reflect about those who were with us for a season and or a reason. They came into our lives and touched us, influenced us, taught us, brought us happiness, and maybe helped us financially. Then they were gone, but never to be forgotten. Think about how you want to be remembered and then start the work on securing the legacy of your life.

Begin by changing the course for the betterment of someone or something; speak up when wrong is apparent against blatant, worldly issues that are inappropriate. Write a letter of significance to affect change in a situation that seems to be going in a compromising direction. But don't forget to celebrate all that you are, and hold on to your family values and upbringing. Embrace all the love that surrounds you as you nurture friendships and fellowships. As Paul wrote, "I thank my God upon every remembrance of you. Always in every prayer of mine for you all making request with joy" (Phil. 1:3–4 KJV). Set aside some time to celebrate and remember the sacrifices of all who paved the way before you, and strive to keep their legacy alive for all to embrace.

CHARACTERISTICS OF GODLY LIVING

The culture by today's standards almost requires that we all be physically fit, energetic, vibrant, good looking, fashion savvy, and financially independent, as well as have the latest devices and be steadily on the go. "For bodily exercise profits a little, but godliness is profitable for all things" (1 Tim. 4:8a NKJV). However, in order to acquire godly living characteristics, we must give reading the Word, prayer, and praise priority in our lives. All those actions will produce an abundant spiritual harvest that consists of happiness, harmony, and forgiveness all of which are wrapped in love. Those characteristics will assuredly cause you to be physically strengthened, mentally equipped, emotionally stable, and trained for endurance to face all the situations you might encounter, with stamina to overcome and be fit for any journey.

We should humbly accept God's pruning, and He surely will prune you at some point in your life, as a requirement to live by His plan and purpose for you. But ultimately, you should devote yourself personally and professionally to the benefit of others, while also serving and giving wherever needed. Then you'll have a plethora of characteristics of godly living for all to see and witness.

CHANGING THE ATMOSPHERE

How can you be a part of the "changing the atmosphere" movement? How will people know we believers are a chosen people set apart if we do not act differently than the world? If we conform to the microwave theory of getting and doing it all right now; if we're prideful and arrogant, don't get what we want, and get upset, angry, moody and depressed; if we're so consumed with posting on social media and taking selfies instead of looking at the broader picture of being part of bettering of the world, how will we effect any change?

We have the power to love unconditionally, to be healed and restored to a spectrum of normalcy, to see a need and fill a deed, to feed the hungry, and to house the homeless. Those actions are linked to changing the atmosphere by adjusting our attitude within ourselves: give a smile instead of a frown, or perhaps give a greeting instead of a complaint. Reach back and help people who have lost their way in life due to uncontrollable circumstances. "Therefore, as we have opportunity, let us do good to all" (Gal. 6:10a ASV). Put on a garment of love, joy, and patience and wear it every day for the greater good while changing the atmosphere for all to observe.

CHOICES

Reflect on the choices you have in a day, a week, a year, or for the rest of your life. There are relationships to consider, the pursuit of a career, getting a degree, or going into the military to serve. Consider whether you want to be a stay-at-home parent and where will you live. What type of car will you drive? How about what to have for dinner tonight? These are seemingly important choices to consider for the betterment in our lives that may change our trajectory, mind-set, attitude, perceptions, and understanding.

We must make the choice to redeem the time we have left to live, because it is precious and won't last forever. Make every effort to recover, buy back, pay off, convert, or discharge—whichever is your choice. Make living and giving paramount in your life. Look for opportunities to tell someone about the goodness of God in your life. Practice listening as well as talking and praying. "Cast your burden on the Lord, and he shall sustain you; he shall never permit the righteous to move" (Ps. 55:22 NKJV). Weigh your options to make the right choices for the right reasons and for the greater good.

CHOOSE TO SERVE

To choose means to take as a choice, to select, to decide or prefer. It also implies an exercise or judgment. To choose means the picking out by preference from what is available, and making an appropriate selection. It's the action of going into the unknown and making a choice of when, where, and how you wish to serve. Perhaps it will be in the military, on a faraway mission field, or maybe it's at a homeless shelter or a food distribution center. You might choose to volunteer in a veterans facility to encourage the wounded toward healing and wholeness. Perhaps you'll tutor youngsters struggling because of too much drama at home and not enough encouragement in their lives.

Wherever you choose to serve, God will surely equip you for the journey. Your character will be exhibited in your obedience, self-control, faith, tireless dedication, and love. "And if it seems evil unto you to serve the Lord, choose for this day whom ye will serve; whether the gods which your fathers served that were on the other side of the flood, or the gods of the Amorites, in whose land ye dwell; but as for me and my house, we will serve the Lord" (Josh. 24:15 KJV). However, be assured that God can choose to use you anytime and anywhere to fulfill His purpose for the kingdom.

CIRCUMSTANCES

Are there conditions, happenings, or events that move in, around, and through your life activities? What do you do with the circumstances that are beyond your control? Certainly life calls for some trials and tribulations. You should rejoice in your circumstances and sufferings, because character is produced through perseverance as well as hope. Maybe you can think about some ways to assist others in their troubled circumstances, such as people with overdue rent, little to no food in the cabinets, or more bills than money at the end of the month. These people may be on the brink of losing hope. Does God know they're troubled? Yes, because He is in all trials and tragedies of life. He either sends them or permits them to happen, but how we respond is up to us.

When we seek to understand that God is present and sovereign in all things, it will give us hope, patience, insight, and guidance in circumstances not of our doing. "And we know that in all things work together for good to them that love God, to them who are the called according to his purpose" (Rom. 8:28 KJV). Therefore, smile, sing, dance with joy in your heart, and believe all your negative circumstances can be worked out for God's purpose in your life.

Closed Doors

What do closed doors represent? Do they have any significance in your life? Could closed doors possibly hide domestic violence, gluttony, jealously, pride, anger, abuse, or perhaps simply disobedience in your life? Sometimes doors are closed to protect you from making the wrong choices in how you deal with what lies within you. It could be to reposition you in another direction away from a misstep, and to maybe teach you perseverance and trust for the long haul.

However, did you ever think about closed doors as an opportunity to go forward and seek some long-forgotten goal or some unintended aspiration you never thought possible, now that the door is miraculously open? Wait for the right moment with a positive attitude, along with a can-do spirit. Journal your thoughts, make a workable plan to undo, and redo some stuff hidden behind your closed doors. Prayer will always help too. Be assured that your closed doors can be opened in due time with a positive outcome so that you can experience wondrous possibilities with a great sense of joy, peace, love, and satisfaction. "I am the door; by me if any man enter in, he shall be saved" (John 10:9a ASV).

CHANGES IN LIFE

We are all set apart by God as prophets to tell others about the Gospel of Jesus Christ and the kingdom of God. "Before I formed you in the womb I knew you, before you were born I sanctified you; I ordained you a prophet to the nations" (Jer. 1:5 NKJV). Where do you want to start, and in which direction do you want your life change quest to pursue? Do you want to be an effective teaching partner who will change people emotionally, mentally, and physically, going through a process from old practices and habits to new realities? Changes in your life might possibly mirror some biblical principles and characters, portraying some life examples in Scripture. You might have to teach someone why change in life is necessary, how it comes about, and how to readily accept it when it occurs.

After learning the basics of change (nothing stays the same), your life might take a new direction, into a totally unexpected position or lifestyle. However, you just might be bold and empower someone to see and demonstrate the need for change beyond themselves and others. Change in life should include their families, neighborhoods, schools, and churches. It should encourage people to embrace all the newness of life changes that they can enjoy forever.

COME OUT OF THE SHADOWS

By definition, a shadow means a darkness; an indistinct or reflected image; a period of gloom, unhappiness, mistrust, doubt; and sometimes a pervasive threat, influence, or atmosphere. Whew, that's a lot! People have a shadow or two in their lives, but some things they would rather keep hidden, like stinky feet, bad breath, or body odor. Serious, life-altering problems such as illicit drugs, alcoholism, pornography, sexual addiction, domestic violence, eating disorder, or some kind of fetish that rules the day needs to come out of the shadows and be dealt with.

You might need to accept professional help to assist you with altering your behavior pattern, as well as medication to calm you in a stressful environment. In the long run, these problems have to be dealt with because they are not healthy and might be life-threatening instead of life-enhancing. "With men it is impossible, but not with God; for with God all things are possible" (Mark 10:27 KJV). If someone has a need to come out of the shadows, encourage them to seek help for a fulfilling lifestyle change of joy, peace, and abundant and everlasting love.

COURAGE

What is courage? It is an attitude of facing and dealing with anything recognized as dangerous, difficult, or painful, instead of withdrawing from it. In 2010, we were all glued to our TVs and watched the rescue of thirty-three miners who had been buried deep inside the earth for sixty-nine days after a mine shaft collapsed. Their will to live and the tenacity of the rescuers to make a way to get them out was pure courage. The situation seemed impossible to accomplish, but God had other plans for these men, their families, their town, and those watching and praying for their survival. After many failed attempts, using various methods of recovery, finally they were miraculously rescued from the darkness of the mine, and they came into the marvelous light above ground. "The things which are impossible with men are possible with God" (Luke 18:27 KJV).

If we stand on God's promises that state "Never will I leave you, never will I forsake you" (Heb. 13:5b KJV) these promises should be enough to propel you forth with immeasurable courage to tell someone about the miraculous results that God has fulfilled in your life. Step out to see a need and fill a deed with bold, uncompromised faith and courage.

DEEP ROOTS

Roots are an anchorage or means of support for the underground part of a seed or plant, an origin, or the source of something. When you want a healthy garden, you tend the soil and provide nutrients, plenty of water, and lots of sunshine. But some weeds or unwanted plants will ultimately grow among the flowers or vegetables you planted. They have to be pulled up by the root, or else they will continue to poke through the soil and overtake your beautiful garden.

Sometimes in your life, deep roots of anger, bitterness, selfishness, jealously, unforgiveness, pride, and ingratitude will invade your beautiful garden of peace. All these attributes will have a grip on your emotions, your attitude, and the decisions and choices you make daily. Your joy is diminished, your patience wears thin, gentleness is rough, faithfulness is compromised, your countenance is saddened, and your goodness and self-control are completely gone, along with your cheerful giving. "Love your enemies, do good to those who hate you, bless those who curse you, and pray for those who spitefully use you" (Luke 6:27–28 NKJV).

Deep roots that have taken over the garden of your life will have to be meticulously dug up so that inappropriate behavior will not keep peeking out any time it wants to. Remember that forgiveness is the key that unlocks the door to freedom, love, joy, and happiness in a healthy, weed-free environment.

DEDICATED

Usually a song, poem, or a celebration is dedicated to a person of achievement. What things in your past have been dedicated, to be handed down through the generations? What's the legacy to be left behind? Is it recipes of favorite foods enjoyed at family gatherings, photos of relatives living far away, writings or thoughts jotted down about events and happenings in the family, or a collection of letters or cards to be displayed? Remain dedicated to let others know about your family—the ups and downs, the ins and outs, and the struggles of life.

But most of all, show how you survived and overcame the wilderness experiences, the joyless days, and the emotional fatigue. "And let us not be weary in well doing; for in due season we shall reap, if we faint not" (Gal. 6:9 KJV). Be mindful that people might need to know about your dedication, love, and perseverance. They also might need to know primarily about the fight to keep your light shining in darkness and not hid in the back of the closet under a pile of clothes.

DON'T SWEAT THE SMALL STUFF

The title is a great slogan that some folks apply to a lot of situations that don't seem to mean much; it's called minutia. There are more important things in life to be concerned about: saneness of mind, the activity of your limbs, hearing, sight, the ability to touch and feel, being able to speak, having laughter, and of course being able to love and have love in return. Also, it's a decent place to live, a job with sufficient income, reliable transportation, enough food to eat, good neighbors, and friends. We have the option in this country, of going to any church, and to worship openly and readily read our Word. Is it worth it to get angry, raise your blood pressure, and maybe get indigestion over something that, if really thought about, might present a very different conclusion?

Why not put your energy, time, talent, and treasure into something worthwhile? Pay it forward on a bill, or buy a bag of groceries for a single mother who used all of her financial resources and has no money left to buy food before the month ends. Help in an after-school tutor program to make sure that no child is left behind. Tell someone about God's goodness, and "Let my mouth be filled with your praise and with your glory all the day" (Ps. 71:8 NKJV).

Do You Have Hope?

Hope in a person, place, or promise—these are all man-made or physical conditions, and they could well be subject to partial or complete failure. However, there are many reasons to hope. There's the hope of winning for your favorite game or team, or the hope of recovery from a surgical procedure or a debilitating illness. There is hope for a smooth transition of buying or selling a house. There is hope for a loving spouse, a good marriage, and obedient children. The list could certainly go on for a while.

But hope in God and the things that matter the most are eternal salvation and the unchanging love of Jesus, plus all the joy that is ours to enjoy. Sometimes we hope for peace and quiet in the midst of a storm. We hope for safety on the freeway to and from work. We assuredly hope for the ability to be mobile one more day. Focus and remember that "Jesus Christ the same yesterday and today and forever" (Heb. 13:8 KJV). Count yourself fruitful and faithful in the hope that the steps that guide you in life are in line with the One, who is always the same, never changes, and gives you everlasting hope.

Do You Have Time?

Time is a measurement that can be about minutes or hours on the clock, a measurement of days in the week, or a distance traveled. Maybe time is a reference to the period that you are doing something significant. But do you have time to live, love, complete a project of your choosing, take a trip or a class, appreciate your spouse and children, and enjoy your job more? The answers are endless. The basic question still remains: Do you have time? Can you help at a food giveaway site, assist an elderly person at the supermarket, attend a Bible study, pray without ceasing, stick to an exercise program, choose to eat healthier foods, and get sufficient rest?

All of these situations denote whether you consider that time is a gift freely given. Time doesn't consider your age or sex, your culture or your circumstances; it's what you do with the time given to you that is most important. "Let nothing be done through selfish ambition or conceit, but in lowliness of mind let each esteem others better than himself" (Phil. 2:3 NKJV). Do the right thing for the right reason, and strive for the right results for the glory of the kingdom. Then you will have time for love, joy, peace and laughter.

DREAMS TO BE REALIZED

Do you have any dreams that could or should be realized but never came to fruition? Dreams are images, ideas, emotions, and sensations that occur in your mind. They could represent a longed-for desire, or an aspiration of something to be realized. Perhaps it's a dream of going to college and obtaining a degree. Maybe it's starting a business after drawing up a plan and securing funding. Possibly it's tutoring or working with kids. Maybe you want a career in politics, law enforcement, the judicial system, or the medical field. Dreams to be realized are anything you want them to be.

With hard work, perseverance, and faith and by allowing God to provide, guide, and protect you, they can be accomplished. "And it shall come to pass in the last days, says God, that I will pour out my Spirit on all flesh; Your sons and your daughters shall prophesy, your young men will see visions, your old men will dream dreams" (Acts 2:17 NKJV). In this twenty-first-century world that is evolving so fast, it is paramount that you be ready to assimilate yourself into the happenings around you. Get prepared to have your dreams to be realized, come to fruition, and culminate in your desired accomplishment of a lifetime.

DRIFTING ALONG AND AWAY

With the change of the seasons, summer seems to be a time of drifting along and away; school is out with lots of outdoor activities planned. Are you going to take advantage of the warm, sunny days to go on a vacation, or to catch up on some home projects like painting, repairing, window washing, and gardening? Whatever it is that you are undertaking, remember to stay connected to the source of life itself. When you feel anxious, lonely, sad, depressed, overwhelmed, or lost, the Word says we can stand on the promises of God. We are able to stand up under trials and tribulations, overcome our enemies, and triumph in persecutions, ridicules, and false accusations. In our sane and sober minds, we can discern with wisdom what our life purpose is, and we don't have to be captive to drifting along and away.

God's love will enable us to hear, believe, hope, and trust in all things. Jesus said, "If you can believe, all things are possible to him who believes" (Mark 9:23 NKJV). When all our powers and faculties are strengthened, regulated, and influenced, then we can speak and act with self-discipline and be anchored with inner peace, power, and love from the cares and woes of this world forever. They will keep us from drifting along and away without any interruption of our life's purpose.

Do You Want to Be Healed?

A lot of people have physical, mental, and emotional conditions that have plagued them from birth, and some conditions are acquired recently from accidents, illness, or work-related injuries. Some people are crippled due to overwhelming challenges from anger, bitterness, rejection, unmet expectations, and unfulfilled dreams from spouses, children, friends, careers, church folks, and finances. Overwhelming life situations will bog you down when you hold onto unforgiven resentment and behavior. They will rob you of your self-esteem and keep you from achieving a healthy and joyous life. They'll even blind you from your identity in Christ.

However, healing is possible if you learn to forgive, stop negative talking, speak life, and believe. Have faith and obedience in permanent healing for yourself and for those around you. "And Jabez called on the God of Israel, saying, Oh that you would bless me indeed, and enlarge my territory, that your hand would be with me, and that you would keep me from evil, that I may not cause pain" (1 Chron. 4:10 NKJV). Yoke obedience, faith, prayer, and your actions together for whatever is in your life that needs to be healed. Keep moving toward the remainder of your life filled with peace, joy, and happiness.

Enjoy Your Journey

Your journey is not about the destination to be reached, but about how and why you enjoy your journey along the way. Go ahead and enjoy the beauty of the flowers that bloomed all summer; partake of all the ripened fruits and vegetables from your garden. However, don't make the mistake of always hurrying so that you don't enjoy the journey down the path of life. Stop to think. When was the last time you had a date with your spouse, made some cookies with your little ones, or had a cup of coffee with your neighbor just to say hi? Have you thought about giving some relief time to a caregiver, checking in on a shut-in, or reading to a sight-impaired person? Have you set aside some time to pray for the homeless, the helpless, and those who can't seem to get it together?

Remember to enjoy your journey to see a need and fill a deed, and at the final destination you will hear, "Commit your way to the Lord, trust also in Him, and He shall bring it to pass" (Ps. 37:3 NKJV). Strive to enjoy the beauty of a sunrise or sunset, the twinkling stars in the sky, ocean waves, mountains and deserts, birds twittering about, and butterflies. There's so much to see on your journey through life, so absolutely enjoy it to the fullest.

EMBRACING CHANGE

Change is often taking, replacing, converting, or substituting one thing for another. Embrace change that happens in our lives, even if it's occasionally for reasons beyond our control or understanding. Maybe there's a career change, a marital situation, a change of money circumstances, a change of living arrangements. Perhaps there's a physical or mental change due to an injury, surgery, or debilitating disease. You will certainly change as you mature and grow older. Embracing change is good if you accept it with obedience and dignity. It is a chance to be challenged and strengthened, to have the ability to stand on your faith and the promises of God and His Word. Everything you encounter is constantly changing, because God is molding, shaping, maturing, and strengthening us for our kingdom journey.

If embracing change is seen as good, then it will surely bring new adventures, new relationships, new attitudes, a new outlook, new points of view, and maybe a new you! "Bless the Lord, O my soul, and forget not all his benefits" (Ps. 103:2 NKJV). Look for opportunities to embrace change—the big and small, some likes and even some dislikes—for the betterment of abundant benefits for a lifetime.

Equipped and Ready

Think about all the situations that seemed to "just happen" in your life. Were you equipped and ready to deal with them? Suppose you could lessen the impact and change the pattern with learned skills that will get you equipped and ready. That might include doing the job and finally getting the project finished, starting a new business, contemplating a career change, and moving into a new house in another city, state, or country. The possibilities are endless, and there is always an opportunity for change or growth. Stand equipped and ready to assist with tutoring after school for those who are lagging behind in their studies. Use some life skills to help someone be able to understand finances, like the concept of saving money.

Teach others nutrition and how to survive and improve the quality of life in a family with more month than money, to get them equipped and ready for life. "Put them in mind to be subject to principalities and powers, to obey magistrates, to be ready for every good work" (Titus 3:1 KJV). All these examples are of someone getting equipped and ready for an improved and enriched lifestyle because you took time to teach, nurture, and equip them for all life has to bring about in one day.

FAITHFULNESS

How much faith is in your life? Do you know that prayer is the key to heaven, but faith is the hinge on the door that swings open into the blessings of God? Your faithfulness is the device used to wait on God for an answer after you have prayed. However, God never expects faith beyond His level of proving His faithfulness to you. Therefore, faith will allow you to maintain your focus by keeping your mind saturated with Scriptures and trusting completely through your doubt. Remember that faith requires an action on your part, so don't ask God to guide you onto the pathway of life if you are not willing to follow His instructions in your answered prayer. Rest assured that your integrity comes from faith in God, and it's also an assurance of what you hope, pray, and stand on. Furthermore, it comes from what is written in God's word that will come to fruition. "We walk by faith, not by sight" (2 Cor. 5:7 KJV).

God will give you inner peace, patience, power, and a love of self as you mature with faith into who He has purposed you to be. God will give you strength for the journey of life that will make you strong as He watches over those who are faithful. He proves His faithfulness in all the prayers He answers, in all the lives and the love He nourishes, and all those He provides for and protects.

FEARS OF MANKIND

The fears of mankind often distress or influence the daily quality of life for some people. Why? First, the unknown is not always a welcome situation; not knowing, what, where, when, or how often paralyzes some people, because they want to know every minute detail before moving forward. Second, the fear of death is not easily thought of or talked about; it seems it's too uncomfortable to even contemplate, especially when it catches us off guard. Third, the fear of failure is not an option in some situations, and falling short of a mark or not being able to measure up to perceived expectations is definitely a fear. Fourth, the fear of betrayal or rejection is to be vulnerable to the trust of someone else's opinion and the outcome. "The Lord is my light and my salvation; whom shall I fear? The Lord is the strength of my life; of whom shall I be afraid? (Ps. 27:1 KJV).

Stand tall and declare that you're not going to be anxious, and that you're going to trust and believe you can overcome and conquer your fears. Speak calmly to yourself in fearful times of distrust, doubt, and despair; lean not on your own understanding. Know without a doubt that you can and will become an overcomer of the fears of mankind, and you will succeed.

FLOWERS

In the spring, when flowers begin to bloom every day, the smell and fragrance are welcome and soothing both to sight and mind. What kind of flower would you like to be? There are so many different species of flowers that it's hard to choose. People also come in different characteristics, cultures, and colors, and together we all bring beauty and fragrance to the garden of the world. Some people are annuals, here to bloom for a short while and then be gone. Some people are perennials that remain in the garden for a long time. Nevertheless, flowers should be planted with the right soil, be watered regularly, get the right amount of sunlight, and be routinely given nutrients. They will thrive if they are weeded, trimmed, and properly cared for.

Our relationships with each other are like flowers in a garden. We thrive to our fullest potential when cultivated with care, concern, and love. "For lo, the winter is past, the rain is over and gone. The flowers appear on the earth; the time of the singing of birds is come" (Song of Sol. 2:11–12a KJV). As you go about tending your garden of communication and connections with your family, your workplace, your neighborhood, and even your church, your relationships will thrive with care and concern, mixed in with lots of goodness, mercy, and patience.

FOCUS, FILLED, AND FAITHFUL

To focus is to pay attention, concentrate, have a clear image. To be filled means to occupy to full capacity, and also to be increased. To be faithful means to be loyal, responsible, obligated, and conscientious. These traits denote people who are living their lives with purpose and intentionality. They have no time for the negativity of life, and they take time to make a difference and sow seeds for change. They volunteer at food distribution centers, provide transportation for someone without a ride, and assist with English as a second language for people who are less educated and bewildered about the customs of this country.

At any moment in our lives, we could be dependent on someone or something to help us move, breathe, and have a decent quality of life. Consider cheerfully giving yourself away to be used to help someone else, and be abundantly blessed while waiting to hear your master say, "Well done, good and faithful servant; you were faithful over a few things, I will make you ruler over many things …" (Matt. 25:21 NKJV). As a result, go about your life focused, filled, and faithful. Watch what happens that will uplift your attitude, finances, and even everyday life situations.

FORGIVENESS

Forgiveness refers to God's pardon of our sins, and it is linked directly to Jesus Christ, who died on the cross for the forgiveness of our sins. Forgiveness is a necessary element directed toward healing, wholeness, restoration, and empowerment. It justifies us, purifies our hearts, removes mountains of guilt from our lives, brings freedom from depression, and dresses us in the necessary armor of God to fight our battles against Satan (Eph. 6:13–17 KJV). God's forgiveness comes with a responsibility and an obligation that demands we forgive others, but first we have to forgive ourselves so we can experience all that He has for us.

We have to forgive rejection for whatever reason it happened, as well as the people and situations that put us in a box of despair. We must forgive when the burden of letting someone continue to hurt us becomes too great to bear. However, when unforgiveness takes away our freedom to serve, share, and give, as well as our joy in the Lord, it's time to seek some answers. When the roots of our problems that flourish are dug up out of the soil of our broken hearts, then the garden of our life is made weed-free, to be filled with the fruit of the Spirit, all wrapped securely in God's love.

Free and Clear with No Strings Attached

Does free and clear mean all of your bills are paid and nothing else is owed? Perhaps you received a gift that didn't require any down payment or repayment. The decisions you have to make require no discussions or intervention, and you will be able to implement the project at any time within reason for your allotted budget—free and clear with no strings attached. However, the greatest freedom comes first in your mind, then in your attitude and in your actions. Freedom comes when you decide to take command of your life you dig out the root of negative memories and attitudes that may cause you to be bound up, afraid, anxious, worried, and not free and clear with no strings attached. "Do not worry about your life" (Matt. 6:25 NIV). "Cast all your anxiety on Him for he cares for you" (1 Pet. 5:7 NIV).

Make every effort to become free of anger, bitterness, sarcasm, and gossip, as well as any other negative characteristics that are not beneficial and pleasing in your life. Be grateful to be free. However, impart to someone else the importance of building up stamina for the long-haul race of life that will ensure eternal freedom with absolutely no strings attached.

FORGE AHEAD

To forge ahead means to give form, shape, reproduce, and move steadily forward against obstacles and difficulties. It's putting in motion an idea, plan, or promise simmering inside of you but not yet brought to fruition. Perhaps it is a new direction or career path that leads into an unknown territory or a risk on your part. Could it be you may need to forge ahead to close some doors on time-consuming, fruitless events; some negative occupational choices; or barren friendships? Maybe it's a lifestyle change of your hair color, weight, dietary habits, and unproductive relationships with relatives. Maybe it's a relocation to another city, state, or country.

When you are motivated to forge ahead, it is done with much prayer, information, and contemplation. These actions are not to get ahead or lag behind, but to stay in step with God's plan for your life, "For God gave us not a spirit of fearfulness; but of power and of love and discipline" (2 Tim. 1:7 ASV). Confidently forge ahead into an unfamiliar world with a new-you attitude, on a new life path, and with an abundance of love, joy, truth, and righteousness. Be free to give yourself away to be used in the kingdom with amazing results and incredible returns.

FREEDOM AND SUBMISSION

Freedom is the resolve of being free from rules, regulations, and patterns. It is an exemption or liberation from the control of another person or an arbitrary power. It's being able to choose or determine your actions without fear, condemnation, or imprisonment. Submission, on the other hand, means to yield or surrender, to trust, and to be obedient; it's a quality of meekness or humility. Freedom involves trust and obedience inside a relationship of love. If your mind has the freedom to give and accept forgiveness, to trust and be trusted, to be healed of past experiences, and to be restored and made functional, then submission is easily obtainable. If your ears and your attitude are open, and if your heart is filled with abundant love to freely give some away, then freedom and submission become daily life practices. "Now the Lord is that Spirit; and where the Spirit of the Lord is there is liberty" (2 Cor. 3:17 KJV).

You will be blessed as you go on a quest to obtain freedom and incorporate submission for God's plan and purpose to work in your life. At the end of the day, practice accepting trust because it leads to freedom and submission, which couples with love and being obedient inside a relationship of peace, patience, and everlasting joy.

FRIENDS

Who and what constitute friends? People may come into your life for a reason, a season, or a lifetime. If they enter for a reason, it is usually for a need that you inwardly prayed for to be met. They might come to assist you through a difficult situation and provide guidance and support. Perhaps they are a tremendous help physically, mentally, or spiritually. But suddenly they are gone; their assignment is finished, so they move on. Perhaps your need has been met, your prayer is answered, your desire is fulfilled, and their work is done.

When people come into your life for a season, it might be your time to grow, share, and learn. They may teach you something new or point you in a totally different direction, such as new traveling adventures or a new hobby. Sometimes they bring an unbelievable amount of joy, but only for a season.

Lifetime relationships teach lifetime lessons, but these friends might be there to jump-start you into a thriving new you. "A merry heart makes a cheerful countenance, but by sorrow of the heart the spirit is broken" (Prov. 15:13 NKJV).

Accept what you have learned from friends of a reason, a season, or a lifetime. Embrace the joy, peace, and love brought anew into your life. Use your lessons learned to bolster other people, amend broken relationships, and spread some joy, peace, and confidence into the world, whether for a season or a lifetime.

FRUIT-BEARING SEASON

When you plant a garden with seeds and then supply nutrients, water, and tender care, you expect a ripening harvest. The fruit maturing in the garden of your life should be joy, peace, patience, kindness, goodness, faithfulness, perseverance, and self-control. Your most abundant harvest in your fruit-bearing season should be overflowing with love. "Beloved let us love one another, for love is of God; and everyone who loves has been born of God and knows God" (1 John 4:7 NKJV). These elements are manifest through God's grace and mercy, which gives energy to faith itself. Your fruit-bearing season is given to you freely by God, perhaps for you to bear the frailties and provocations of others without murmuring and complaining. "God created the Heavens and the Earth" (Gen. 1:1 NIV). He provides the rain and the sun to make a harvest grow in due season.

Therefore, as you faithfully and lovingly assess how blessed you are, go about tending your garden, Pull some weeds and prune some vines, if necessary, for a great harvest that will manifest abundant fruit throughout your fruit-bearing life. Display an attitude pleasing to God, and give Him thanks for your abundance.

GOD'S PEACE

Everything the world has to offer us is incorporated in "the lust of the flesh, and the lust of the eyes, and the pride of life, these are not of the Father, but is of the world" (1 John 2:16 KJV). These conditions are incapable of giving the peace that the soul needs, the peace that passes all understanding, or everlasting peace. Fame, fortune, and false religion do not quiet the voice of conscience and take away sin, and neither do they reconcile us back to God. However, Jesus gives us peace because He is the author, promoter, and keeper of peace. Peace is reconciliation and love—peace with God and the peace of God. Its peace with one another, peace in your own spirit, peace of mind, and peace of who you are in Christ. Almighty peace all comes from our justification before God, given to us through Jesus.

"My peace I leave with you, my peace I give to you; not as the world gives do I give to you. Let not your heart be troubled, neither let it be afraid" (John 14:27 NKJV). As a result, forgiveness brings peace to a troubled soul, and it allows the fruit of the Spirit to grow and be manifested in your life. God's peace fills you and prepares you, so you can give to others and live an abundant life free from worry and fear, with the everlasting assurance of peace in your life.

GETTING INVOLVED

Getting involved means to be connected or committed, to occupy, and to relate. It means employing some action regarding a project or a situation. It's going the extra mile to finish a project in your neighborhood or church. It means encouraging someone with low self-esteem to live up to their potential and to use your knowledge to teach English as a second language. Getting involved in the political process means registering potential voters, passing out literature, and assisting at the polls. Getting involved also means listening when someone needs a sounding board, be it sympathy or empathy. Involvement could mean reading to someone with failing eyesight, or speaking life to someone who is homeless and perhaps hopeless in a situation. Getting involved might be cooking a meal or visiting someone who recently had surgery and has a long recovery process. Get involved with mentoring a new mother who seems to be overwhelmed by her changed situation.

Getting involved is the act of giving unconditionally. "And there you shall eat before the Lord your God, and you shall rejoice in all to which you have put your hand, you and your households, in which the Lord your God has blessed you" (Deut. 12:7 NJV). As you go about getting involved in as many activities as are applicable for you, it will be an encouragement for those less fortunate who desperately need your input.

GIVING

What should your attitude toward giving in uncertain economic times reflect? *First*, have a thankful attitude that you even have something to give, when so many others have even less. Second, giving demonstrates love, care, and concern; let the goodness of your life flow outward. Third, practice the principle of sowing and reaping: "He who sows sparingly will also reap sparingly, and he who sows bountifully will also reap bountifully" (2 Cor. 9:6 NKJV). Fourth, giving can make it possible that the needs of others may be met with your sacrificial giving. Remember that giving does not always mean money; it could mean giving your time to tutor students in need of extra homework explanation and help. Give your talent, assisting with a school play or a community project. Volunteer at a senior living home as a chaperone on outings.

Giving is imitating God, who is the giver of life; He gives out of His love for His creation, and He has demonstrated "…for God loves a cheerful giver." (2 Cor. 9:7b NIV). He gave us Jesus, who paid the penalty for our sins. When you give thankfully, faithfully, and cheerfully, it becomes an opportunity to demonstrate your love by blessing God and being a blessing to His people. Allow an attitude of giving to demonstrate for the world to see the richness and blessings of your life flowing outward.

Go Along to Get Along

What does it mean to go along to get along? It means to not speak up in a degrading situation, because you don't want to seem like a snitch. Perhaps you do not act, allowing drug activity and family abuse to continue without going to the proper authorities. You don't stop and listen when children speak about bullying taking place in their school. You go along with public opinion and the status quo, keeping things as they are because change may be overwhelming and unacceptable to certain people. Remembering the quote from Edmund Burke, "the only thing necessary for the triumph of evil is for good men to do nothing" and they seem to go along to get along. Sometimes people don't want to make waves; they are comfortable where they are and would rather blend in. "Watch and pray, that you enter not into temptation; the spirit indeed is willing, but the flesh is weak" (Matt. 26:41 ASV).

Going along to get along for the right reasons could be to display integrity, moral uprightness, purity, and honesty. You can do the right thing at the right time and for the greater good. Realize that you are blessed and are appointed to be a light in darkness, a sweet scent in an unpleasant and odorous atmosphere, and salt to flavor life. Truly believe that you don't have to go along to get along. Simply be yourself and live life abundantly, and let God do the rest.

GOD'S GOODNESS

The word *goodness* means the state or quality of being good, the best part or the valuable element of a thing; it is excellence, kindness, or benevolence. Goodness is an attribute of God. When He interacts with us, He is being good even when we merit nothing from Him. Look back on your life and reflect on some thoughts about the goodness of God and all He has done for you. It is written and taught throughout the Bible that the goodness of God is the thrust behind the blessings that He bestows upon us daily. The cause of God's goodness is in Himself, and we are the recipients of His goodness without merit, favor, or reward. God is not concerned about our worldly attributes or accumulations, but about our righteousness, joy, love, and kindness; our witnessing; and what we do for the kingdom.

It is remarkable to know that our weaknesses are turned into strengths by the goodness of a loving God, "Surely goodness and love will follow me all the days of my life, and I will dwell in the house of the Lord forever" (Ps. 23:6 NIV). Therefore whenever we feel depressed, lonely, anxious, or lost, the Word says we can count on all the goodness received from God. He will enable us to get through to the next achievement in our lives, a level of growth, maturity, and understanding with much love, to sow seeds for change and make a difference in the world.

Get to Know Your Neighbor

We are truly blessed in this country, and we all should be thankful. But in a world that is growing more troubled and chaotic each day with recent events, it's paramount that we get to know our neighbors, or anyone living in close proximity to or around us. Do you know your children's playmates and their parents, or the teachers at their school? Do you know anyone in your neighborhood who is physically handicapped and needs assistance with household chores? Is a single mother struggling to hold her family together with meager resources from a bare-bones education, a divorce, or some other negative event in her life? Is an after-school program in your neighborhood in need of reliable people to facilitate a safe, caring environment for the advancement of children's mental, physical, and intellectual maturity?

We all need to move out of our comfort zones, get to know our neighbors, and be more attentive to what's happening around us. We never know if or when an occasion will arise that we might need the assistance of our neighbors, so we should get to know them, enjoying a new friendship or a renewed acquaintance. Be mindful to "love your neighbor as yourself" (Luke 10:27b NKJV).

GRATEFUL

Grateful is a feeling of appreciation, satisfaction, and being thankful. Be grateful to be, to do, and to have no matter the situation, whether in need or in abundance. Each day, make and implement a plan with the gift of your time, talent, and treasure wherever you go. Traveling and experiencing different cultures, climates, ethnic groups, and lifestyles will broaden your life perspective. As you are exposed to life itself, learn to be grateful for all you have and the freedoms you have inherited. "Delight yourself in the Lord and he will give you the desires of your heart" (Ps. 37:4 NIV).

Speak a word of encouragement to someone in a down-and-out situation, or simply smile and say hello. Do a random act of kindness without expecting any return on your investment. Most of all, be grateful for all the Lord has blessed you with: activity of your limbs; saneness of mind; freedom to live, work, and play wherever you like or can afford; and freedom to worship and read the Word out in the open. Go back and reclaim the heritage and your culture that have been so graciously given to you, and be grateful to freely express and enjoy them forevermore. Absorb the belief that if you give yourself away to be used, you might find there are more situations to be grateful for then you ever imagined.

GOD'S LOVE AND PROMISES

Reflect back on your life and some of the promises you made. Perhaps they have not yet manifested in your life. Sometime when you feel lonely, not quite focused, depressed, anxious, or lost, remember that the Word says you can stand on the promises of God and His love. He has given you the power to encounter danger and despair, to bear up under trials and tribulations, and to triumph in persecutions—all while under the banner of His love. In your sane and sober mind, you can discern with prudence and wisdom, seeing things in their proper perspective, the right proportions, and the proper relations. God's love enables you to hear, believe, hope, and endure all things. Finally, when your soul is harmonized, regulated, and influenced, then you will be able to think, speak, and act with self-discipline.

God is love, and He has given us an inner peace, power, and love of self so that we can mature into who He has purposed us to be. "And this is the promise which he promised us, even eternal life" (1 John 2:25 ASV). Allow yourself to experience the fullness of God's love and promises. Freely give away some love to people in need so that they can keep going down the path of life.

HAPPINESS IS A CHOICE

Happiness is a feeling. It is having or showing great pleasure, being favored by circumstances, being fortunate, and having contentment. It's a choice we make when faced with situations or activities we had nothing to do with, even if we didn't plan them, didn't want them, and would prefer not to be involved with them. We have the option of having happiness in our lives every day with our spouse, with our children, in our community, and in our place of worship.

Each of us was created unique to our purpose and place, to use our twenty-four hours to abundantly live our lives and count for something. We are free to make a choice to send a card, call a friend just to say hello, have lunch with a sick person, or tutor youngsters struggling with math or reading. It is our right to do so! Happiness is a choice to be content with what you have and who you are. It's a choice of what you do or say, and how you act toward others; it's called attitude. "Let your conversation be without covetousness; and be content with such things as ye have, for He hath said, I will never leave thee, nor forsake thee" (Heb. 13:5 KJV). Let some happiness and lots of joy overflow into the world and onto other people. It won't cost you anything, but it will make you a richer person if you make happiness your choice every time.

Hard on Ourselves

Why are we so hard on ourselves? We are all made in the image of God: pure, loved, and blessed. So what went wrong on our life paths that we seem to have the perception that we're not worthy, smart, pretty, wealthy, young, thin, or rich enough? We're spending so much time on the negative aspects of our lives, and we push the positives right out of our minds, hearts, and attitudes. The onus seems to be on those who are young, pretty, thin, wealthy, popular, and proud. Wrong! We have forsaken our first love and turned our lives into a daily hush and rush performance. Could it be that we are hard on ourselves because we may know better, but we are not doing better? We seem to be patterning our life to reflect who we desire to be, not who we are right now.

Stop and think for a moment about all that you already have, what you do with what you have, and where you go with what you have. Are you hard on yourself? These are some random thoughts and reminders to ponder, "As also in all his epistles, speaking in them of these things, in which are some things hard to understand, which untaught and unstable people twist to their own destruction" (2 Pet. 3:16c NKJV). Soften up, love yourself more, and begin to enjoy life and all your surroundings.

HOLD ON AND DON'T GIVE UP

What do you do when you seem to not be moving forward, and the future looks dim? Perhaps your company has laid off several people, and your workload has increased, so your promotion is definitely not forthcoming. The bank sent a statement and doubled their fees on your already dwindling funds. The utility companies sent notices that rate hikes are necessary. Gasoline prices at the pump keep increasing, and your car insurance premiums have increased. Food and clothes are more expensive. School tuition keeps going up, student loans are due, and your children have been caught up in worldliness and disobedience through social media. What do you do to hold on until times get better? And what if they *don't* get better?

"I have been young, and now am old; yet have I not seen the righteous forsaken, nor his seed begging bread" (Ps. 37:25 KJV). Isn't it amazing how an access route will be closed, or we are detoured and have to navigate another way by our faith and obedience until we find an opening or an opportunity? These are times of challenge and change. Look for your resources in the Lord, no matter how bleak the situation. Recognize that if God guides you on your way, surely He will provide all you need, and pray that you will be changed through your life challenges if you hold on, don't give up, and know that hope is everlastingly eternal.

HAVE COURAGE TO CHANGE

Do you have courage to change? Your life changes could possibly include your profession, your mate, your siblings, and community involvement. Perhaps a change would involve relocation to another city, state, or country. Maybe it's your own attitude, behaviors, or mannerisms that need change from the usual way of doing things. Perhaps you need a tune-up or a timeout? Challenges in life will force the courage to change to come up to the surface, and then real action will materialize.

Initially, courage to change starts with a decision; you have to formulate and diligently stick to a suitable plan. Don't forget to reward yourself for your achievements and accept new unfamiliar feelings and some failures. However, don't beat yourself up if you're not making tremendous strides—small steps are always welcome. It will be beneficial for you to latch onto an accountability partner, who will uplift and assist you with your courage to change, no matter what it entails. "Therefore do not worry about tomorrow, for tomorrow will worry about its own things" (Matt. 6:34a NKJV). Keep a journal of the progress of your "courage to change" regimen that has matured into a new and fulfilled you, and share with others your changed outlook.

HONESTY

What is honesty, and what does it mean to you? It is defined as being truthful and fair; having integrity; freedom from lying, stealing, or cheating; and an incorruptible sense of self. Honesty doesn't mean to go along to get along, and it certainly does not mean to cut corners to make the project work. Neither does it mean to do something or act out while nobody is looking. It means to be the same person whether one's being watched or left alone. It means to stand up and speak out against injustice, even if no one else supports the issue. It means doing the right thing!

Could honesty actually mean making a difference if seeds of freedom from corruption or positive moral character traits are displayed and implemented? Remember that corruption or sin is not just murder and mayhem—it is chaos that is deeply entwined into our lives. Subsequently, we may not even realize the decisions or the consequences of our actions. The unbelief, wickedness, exploitation, and ungodliness of the world also plays a part that creeps slowly into our lives through the establishment of social media, television, movies, and music. "We then that are strong ought to bear with the infirmities of the weak, and not to please ourselves" (Rom. 15:1 KJV). With fortitude, go ahead and brighten the environment around you with some honesty and integrity. Mix in some perseverance and peace with it while you're at it.

Honoring Mothers

A mother has a special place in your heart. Whether she is a grandmother, auntie, sister, female teacher, or a neighbor, all are women who have so lovingly contributed something to your life. What things in the past have been set aside to be handed down through generations? What is the legacy to be left behind? Is it property or a family homestead, memories of family gatherings, or a certain promise made to be fulfilled on a certain day or event, perhaps it's a tree planted in memory of a departed loved one? Whatever the family journey, let folks know about you and your entire household. There are definitely lessons to be gleaned from the ups and downs, ins and outs, and struggles of life.

Convey to others how your family overcame some of their negative experiences, some joyless days that were filled with fear, fatigue, and worry. Someone else may need to know about and be encouraged by the dedication and perseverance of all the women who poured something into your life. Tell them about the nurturing love of your mother, the prayers of your grandmother, and the concern of your auntie. "Her children rise up, and call her blessed; her husband also, and he praises her" (Prov. 31:28 NKJV). Lastly, tell all the women you know how much you love and appreciate them for pouring into your life, as well as the remembrance for someone else to gain knowledge and wisdom to bless all the mothers in his or her life.

How to Handle Suffering

Suffering means to feel distress or something unpleasant; to endure pain, injury, or a loss. Some people are clever at hiding the issues that cause suffering and its effects on their lives. Society wants to drug or medicate it, surgically get rid of it, divorce it, institutionalize it, or kill it. How you handle suffering should be an attempt to ascertain what has got you bound up and unable to straighten out your life situations. Suffering often comes when you are at a low point in your life. It might help if you journal your thoughts and feelings for clues related to what is happening in your life. Read the Word, which will give you abundant spiritual fruit to nourish and encourage you. As you pray, praise Him and sing to yourself to overcome and lift your inner spirit onto the healing side of life. "Yet in all these things we are more than conqueror through Him who loves us" (Rom. 8:37 NKJV).

The weeding out and elimination process is to mentally equip you with strength, endurance for the long haul, stamina to overcome, and satisfaction to know you can be fit for any journey. Position yourself whenever or wherever needed for the benefit of others as you daily demonstrate how to handle suffering and be an overcomer with dignity, love, and joy.

INTEGRITY: THE WAY
TO GOD'S BEST

What is integrity, and what does it mean to us? It is ethical soundness, purity, and honesty that encompasses our entire moral character. It has special reference to uprightness in any financial, judicial, or medical dealings. In other words, integrity should be the utmost in any type of mutual business transaction for others. It is also defined as honesty, truth, completeness, and dependability that culminates in an unbroken situation with a sense of excellence.

Integrity comes from faith in God and the reverence of God, and so lack of integrity comes from falling away and disavowing all beliefs in God. Operating in integrity is a decision we make daily—whether to be a person of honor and be true to our word and understanding. Integrity affects so many aspects of our daily lives, and it keeps us protected in our full armor of God so that our needs are supplied and our seed is multiplied. "The fear of the Lord is the beginning of wisdom, and knowledge of the Holy One is understanding" (Prov. 9:10 NKJV). Let your integrity be as natural as the breath of life is to you. Allow the integrity of doing the right thing and your trust and uprightness to be boldly displayed in all your activities of daily living.

Investments

The stock market and its myriad of investments seem to be stable for now, but it is still subject to ups and downs at a moment's notice. Consider some of the investments you have already made. Perhaps they're educational investments as you seek to upgrade yourself to a better position within your job or company, or you're studying to further your career path. Physical investments are for your body: eat for nutrition, take vitamins to stave off some effects of aging and replenish essential body minerals, and exercise to stay flexible and decrease some effects of aging. Mental investments keep your mind massaged and focused to respond appropriately and forestall forgetfulness. Relational investments are top priority for friendships, because we need to speak into others' lives, and we need them to whisper in our ears as well.

The investment of giving and servicing seem to go a long way in preparing us for whatever investment God has for us. "But seek ye first the kingdom of God, and His righteousness; and all these things will be added unto you" (Matt. 6:33 KJV). Regardless of what the stock market does or doesn't do, whether the housing crisis rises or falls, and whether the corporate world spends lavishly and the workers get only the basics, remember that we have to stand on the investments we have already been granted—life, liberty, and the pursuit of happiness, which all come from the will of God and flow outward and into the purpose for our lives.

IS IT OUR RESPONSIBILITY?

Whether you go to early church, Saturday church, or Sunday church, or a synagogue or a temple, you have a responsibility in what is happening now and in the future of your faith and where you worship. Our churches are in trouble, enrollment is declining, and every day congregants seem to be unsure how to biblically integrate anger, sadness, resentment, and other emotions in their lives. They seem to be defensive and incapable of revealing their weaknesses, and they appear to be threatened by or intolerant of different viewpoints. They are zealous about ministering at church but are blind to their spouses' loneliness at home. They are so involved in "serving" that they fail to take care of themselves. Without proper organization in a church, many facets of discipleship are lost. Some churches spend lots of money on evangelism and only small amounts on administration to maintain a system for those who have been added and need to be discipled to maturity.

Is it our responsibility? Yes. We need to step up our participation, get involved, and not wait for others to complete a task or assignment. Remember that the church belongs to God, and we are all included in His plan for the kingdom. "For the time will come when people will not put up with sound doctrine. Instead, to suit their own desires, they will gather around them a great number of teachers to say what their itching ears want to hear" (2 Tim. 4:3 NIV). Is it our responsibility to uphold the main principles and beliefs of the church? I think all would agree that yes, it definitely is!

It's the Little Things That Count

It's the little things in life that count for so much. The little things seem to get other things going and accomplished in ways we don't even notice. But what are the little things that are so integrated into our everyday lives? Showing love to folks with a smile and a "Hello, how's your day?" attitude. Forgiving and forgetting is a little thing, but sometimes we make it so overwhelming that it seems like an insurmountable task. Perhaps it's giving some of your time to tutor a student to succeed in school, or writing a letter of concern on a neighborhood issue that requires some clarification and resolution. Maybe it's asking corporations for donations for homeless facilities, and providing funds to feed the needy.

I'm sure if you look around, there are a plethora of little things to be attended to—and it's the little things that count. Often I need to pray, Lord make me an instrument to handle what needs to be done and allow me to never tire of doing the right thing. So get involved in the actions or the conclusions of reactions to big situations that seem to lack a favorable outcome. It's the little things that count, and they have to be tackled and brought to a favorable outcome in order to benefit everyone. This premise should keep them from blowing up into an issue with no end.

JUST ASK

If you want to know something, look it up in a reference book or a commentary, or simply ask someone for the information you seek. Many people don't want to ask someone due to pride, poor spelling or grammar, low self-esteem, or other lowered life expectations, and so they don't ask. Some people might think you're a dummy, and they might think that you should have already learned some things, but nobody knows everything. How about the premise when you meet people and ask if they would like prayer for an issue in their lives, or asking whether they are saved? Ask seniors if they need a ride to a doctor's appointment or to the grocery store. Ask if you can be signed on as an after-school tutor for students struggling to comprehend reading or math. Ask if you can relieve a stay-at-home mom so she can have some time for herself.

Remember that asking works both ways, and there are a lot of issues that could be overcome if people would simply step out of their comfort zone and ask. "Ask, and it will be given to you; seek, and you will find; knock, and it will be opened to you. For everyone who asks receives, and he who seeks finds, and to him that knocks it will be opened" (Matt. 7:7–8 NKJV). As a result, do not be surprised when you receive a response from people with discernment and wisdom that has grown and matured in them just by their asking.

JUST IN TIME

"Just in time" is the relationship of the rightful, proper, balanced, or measurable intervals that span a period of activity in our lives. "Just in time" is a reasonable time or experience when events transpire in your life without planning, circumstance, or an unknown outcome. Time is the point at which something is happening, has happened, or will happen to us or for our benefit, and over which we often have no control. "Just in time" to appreciate your spouse, your children, and your home life for a healthy peaceful existence. "Just in time" for a career change or job interview, moving to a new state, or perhaps entering a new relationship. "Just in time" to avoid a life-threatening medical crisis, or to quit an addiction that has a long time stranglehold on you. Maybe "just in time" to avert a financial or mental breakdown, or to save a young person from going down the absolute wrong road with the wrong people. "To everything there is a season, and a time to every purpose under heaven" (Eccles. 3:1 KJV).

However, you should be diligent about planning and implementing your daily activities to cut down on the stress so that no surprises creep up on you. Enjoy your "just in time" life experiences with lots of gusto and joy. When everything is working in harmony, step back and take pleasure in the overflowing and explosive productivity in your life that came just in time.

JUST SAY NO

It is easy to just say no. Sometimes it's rather hard to do, but it takes practice to say and mean it. What makes it so hard to say it and not do it? Is it our lifetime habits, our self-consumed pride, and our "I'm going to get mine first" attitude? Those are not mature, productive behaviors—in fact, they are negative and unhealthy. The "just say no" campaign from a few years ago was an answer to the drugs that had begun to permeate the country and influence young people and those weak to other elements. It is imperative to say no not only to drugs but to unhealthy eating, minimal exercise, not enough sleep, not enough time spent with one's spouse or children, and one's community projects.

Be proactive and consciously work to turn your "just say no" into a yes with a more fulfilling lifestyle. Declare how grateful you are for life itself, for the ability to see, hear, speak, and function with a sane and sober mind, for the ability to discern with understanding and to "just say no" to inappropriate situations. It takes about three weeks to break a habit and reinforce a new one. Realize that if good people do nothing, evil spreads in the land, and that robs us of our ability to lead a life of honesty, integrity, and truthfulness in order to be productive, healthy, and happy. Remember that "Yet in all these things we are more than conquerors through him who loved us" (Rom. 8:37 NKJV). We have the power to stand up and just say no!

KNOWLEDGE VERSUS WISDOM

Knowledge is the act of knowing, facts, figures, memories, and all that has been perceived or grasped by our minds. It can be concluded that knowledge is everything we have learned or experienced throughout our lifetimes. It is stored information to be sorted, read, used, or recalled at some future time. However, think about what we are expected to do with all the knowledge we have access to through the Internet, Facebook, Twitter, and other avenues of instant, worldwide opinions and viewpoints.

On the other hand, wisdom is what we do with the information we have acquired or stored up in our memories. Discernment is the key that will unlock understanding in your life and the categorization of all your acquired knowledge to use for the betterment of life in the kingdom. You can rightly combine it together to assist with an after-school tutoring program or in a class to assist students with their English as a second language. Perhaps offer to read or write letters for someone who is blind or handicapped; schedule a day to help with senior citizen shopping. Why not share your knowledge and wisdom with other individuals so that they may become more familiar with the customs and culture of this country? "If any of you lacks wisdom, let him ask of God, who gives to all liberally and without reproach, and it will be given to Him" (James 1:5 NKJV).

LIVING BY THE SPIRIT

Living by the Spirit signifies a continuous, habitual interaction with the Holy Spirit who, because of our salvation, lives in us. It means being under His submission, conviction, authority, and direction in your life, rather than having your own interpretation. "God is Spirit, and those who worship Him must worship in spirit and truth" (John 4:24 NKJV). The end result of living by the Spirit is having a life filled with power for living, leading, loving, serving, and witnessing.

However, before you can claim power to "do all things through Christ who strengthens you" (Phil. 4:13 NKJV), you must empty yourself of anger, selfish ambitions, sexual immorality, self-seeking pleasures of the world, pride, envy, and the worship of other gods. The overflow of living by the Spirit in your life is the evidence that frees you to worship God, study the Word, help mature and effectively equip other saints for ministry, evangelize the good news of Jesus Christ, build up His Church, and prepare for the kingdom to come. As you learn to listen to your inner voice inside of you, you can make a commitment to do the right thing, with a plan and a purpose for living by the direction of the Spirit living within you.

LOOKING AND DOING YOUR BEST

Are you looking and doing your best today and every day? That means a smile instead of a frown or a worried scowl on your face. Are you a friendly person who speaks to everyone who passes by you, and who freely gives compliments to others? Do you invite conversation and make a person feel comfortable in an unfamiliar situation? However, looking and doing your best requires practice with diligence; the more you do it, the more natural it will feel.

Focus on your strengths and help others get strong. Remember to stay positive and open yourself up to the world. Laugh out loud, put a song on your lips and in your heart, love life, and don't be afraid to shine your light into the darkness around you. Be assured that you are looking and doing your best to extend yourself out into an unknown world. Your attitude will show others that you are a person full of love, joy, kindness, and goodness, with a willingness to extend friendship and let the goodness of God show forth through your life. "Let no one despise your youth, but be an example to the believers in word, in conduct, in love, inspirit, in faith, in purity" (1 Tim. 4:12 NKJV).

LOVE NEVER FAILS

Do you know that love never fails in the long run? Some things, events, situations, relationships, and perhaps people might fail, but not love! Love never fails to build friendships in order to show itself as friendly to others. Love never fails to forgive, build up the broken-hearted, heal hidden wounds, restore wholeness, and make a difference. Love is a powerful force that can change the destiny of lives and plot new courses of action. Love can provide the reason to live for the hopeless, homeless, and physically challenged. Think about all the things love can do to make your family, neighborhood, community, workplace, and even your church a joyous, open, and welcoming environment.

"And you shall love the Lord your God with all your heart, with all your soul, and with all your mind and with all your strength. You shall love your neighbor as yourself" (Mark 12:30–31a NKJV). Go forth and embrace love, and make it a permanent demonstration in your life. Most of all, realize the fact that love never fails and conquers pain, guilt, heartache, sorrow, depression, and rejection, as well as anything else you cannot handle.

LIVING SACRIFICES

Are you a living sacrifice? Exactly what does that mean? What is your part and purpose? We are supposed to be sacrificing ourselves for service to God and mankind. It simply means to give ourselves away so we can be used. We should have a mind-set to be available, willing, humble, and equipped to serve where, when, and however we're needed. "I beseech you therefore, brethren by the mercies of God, that you present your bodies a living sacrifice, holy, acceptable to God, which is your reasonable service" (Rom. 12:1 NKJV).

However, your sacrifices do not mean giving up French fries with a hamburger, or a piece of chocolate cake after dinner. Perhaps your sacrificing might mean giving up TV viewing for reading the Bible, or serving in church or at a community function before spending the day at the mall or the beach. It could mean sharing your faith and telling someone about the goodness in your life. Maybe a sacrifice means to surrender yourself totally to God's will and be in the world, but not of the world. Consider that the sacrifices you give up will make you slimmer, leaner, and trimmer, more like God purposed you to be. You'll be a living sacrifice for the greater good and a great example and motivation to everyone.

LOVE YOUR NEIGHBOR AS YOURSELF

Who are your neighbors, and why love them as yourself? A neighbor could be an acquaintance, friend, nearby relative, or the person who lives next door or around the corner. Treat your neighbors with respect, even if they're a different sex, religion, culture, or ethnicity. Be grateful for neighbors who might also look out for you if the need arises. Focus on the relationship for all the good and benevolent situations that might grow throughout the years. Take time to get to know your neighbor for the various resources hidden within them. Follow your instincts to love your neighbor as yourself, and watch a life unfold in abundance and joy.

Everyone wants to have a friend, but some people don't know how to process the steps to have one, so it starts with you and neighborly love. You'll enjoy life and have it more abundantly, and you'll have healing, wholeness, and restoration in your families, marriages, children, schools and churches, and yourself. "Let each one of you speak truth with his neighbor; for we are members of one another. Be angry and do not sin, do not let the sun go down on your wrath, nor give place to the devil" (Eph. 4:25–27 NKJV).

Mission Impossible

How would you handle an impossible mission? Did you overcome and move on with your sanity and safety intact? The Apostle Paul was especially chosen by God for a mission impossible: to bring the Gospel to the churches in Corinth, Galatia, Ephesus, Philippi, and Colossae. With prayer, praise, and thanksgiving, he worked to complete the assignment given to him with a clear sense of divine purpose and calling. Paul had an unshakable conviction with divine authority, and he had a constant spirit of dependence on Him. Paul was assigned a difficult, impossible mission to complete.

Sometimes in life, you might want to give up, hide from the task handed to you, and run away. On the other hand, your assigned mission might seem impossible, unfair, or too time consuming. But Paul worked to instruct the believers in knowledge and faith, as well as encourage the Jews and Gentiles to work together as one body in Christ. Paul's life was characterized by an unbending dedication to complete the impossible mission bestowed upon him on the Damascus Road (Acts 9:3–6). We learn that "Happy is the man who finds wisdom, and the man who gains understanding" (Prov. 3:13 NKJV).

Motivated to Move

If you are motivated to act or move in a particular direction, should you stop to question, or should you attempt to figure out the reason for the demand? Did you just get involved with a project or a situation without some kind of projected outcome? In reality, did you make a solid plan or a sketch of the project with a completed timeline before securing all your materials? All these actions are important in the motivation and implementation of ongoing activities in your life. Whether you are involved with planning a cruise, buying a new car, obtaining a mortgage for a home, or moving to another neighborhood, these situations require some rational motivation with a thoroughly thought-out plan of action to be successful in your endeavor, and with a certain degree of energy and resolve to move forward.

Additionally, there is always something to do to move ahead to secure your home, your career, or your family and their safety, so get in line and be motivated to move for the good of all involved. "You will show me the path of life; in your presence is fullest of joy; at your right hand are pleasures forevermore" (Ps. 16:11 NKJV). Be encouraged to move in some unknown situations with unaware actions, and let the outcome be your final reward.

MORAL AND SOCIAL CONDUCT

Moral and social conduct seem to be changing our lifestyles every day. The family structure has eroded; the divorce rate and single-parent households are increasing; and alcohol, drugs, gambling, and abusive sex have risen at alarming rates. Social media has changed some of our basic forms of communication. The dress code is almost nonexistent, and biblical guidelines and Christian principles have been compromised for a relaxed lifestyle that caters to man's pleasures rather than God's will.

What would Jesus do? It's a good point to ponder as we examine, interject, and initiate our personal ethics beyond our finite understanding and into a plan of action against immorality. It is imperative that we stand and declare our position on issues that are individually selfish, morally reckless, and socially destructive, and that negatively impact our families, schools, churches, and communities. Be aware and realize that evil prevails when good men do nothing. "For what is a man profited, if he shall gain the whole world, and lose his own soul?" (Matt. 16:26a KJV). Realistically think about how you can make a difference and sow seeds for change as you encounter situations throughout your day. How can they be made better or changed for the good of a moral and socially conscious lifestyle?

More Is Needed

Recent global events have us wondering where we are going, and whether we are going to make things change for the better. There is racial profiling of less desirable people, indiscriminate bombings and senseless killings, homeless refugees forced out of their homeland, cultural differences, and war. There are floods, droughts, crop failures, tornadoes, unseasonable weather, and unpredictable travel and flight schedules. People are physically, mentally, and spiritually burdened and overwhelmed, and it seems that more is needed in their daily lives.

Turn off the TV. Take some time out to play some games with the family, socialize, and catch up with what's happening within your circle of friends. Stop to think that more is needed as we walk down the path of life. We need to love more, hug more, laugh more, seek out an opportunity to help more, give of ourselves more regarding our time, talent, and treasures. We need to be thankful for the things we do have, the people in our lives, and the freedoms we have. But still more love and forgiveness is needed, and more prayer is definitely needed. Remember that "God so loved the world that he gave His only begotten son, that whoever believes in Him should not perish but have everlasting life" (John 3:16 NKJV).

MOVING FORWARD

Hopefully we are moving forward as a united nation and as human beings. We should be moving forward past divided differences, unmet expectations, unresolved issues, failed relationships, and unforgiven or forgotten friendships. We should definitely be moving out of disappointment, depression, and the despair of life. We're moving because of the fruit of the Spirit that resides in us, and that is love, joy, peace, kindness, patience, goodness, faithfulness, gentleness, and self-control (Gal. 5:22–23).

We're moving forward because it's the right thing to do, to influence, encourage, and lift up others and help them on their way. We're moving forward because we can make a difference as we sow seeds for change, for the betterment of our existence. "See then that you walk circumspectly, not as fools but as wise, redeeming the time, because the days are evil" (Eph. 5:15–16 NKJV). Therefore be blessed as you move forward with great expectations into unexplored territory. Whether it's a new career, a relationship, a new marriage, a new location, a new attitude, or a new way of doing something, try it, and just maybe it will work for you on your quest of moving forward into your new destiny.

Murmuring and Complaining

Lots of things happen in our lives over which we have absolutely no control. The car didn't start in the morning, or on the way to work, someone cut you off on the freeway. The elevator isn't working, so you have to walk up to the twelfth floor. The copy machine ran out of ink before your major presentation is due. Murmuring denotes anger and discontent, whereas complaining leads to a hardening of your heart with an attitude that will lead to turning away from God—and who will you silently talk to after you have turned away? "So, do all things without murmuring and disputing; that ye may be blameless and harmless, the sons of God" (Phil. 2:14–15a KJV).

Enjoy all the plentiful blessings showered upon you, and rejoice in the newness of each day. Wake up and be grateful for your eyesight, hearing, mobility of your limbs, and saneness of your mind. Enjoy your friendships and the people with whom you fellowship. Cherish your salvation and the promises that come from God: He'll never leave us or forsake us, no weapon formed against us shall prosper, He'll supply all our needs, we are promised victory over death, His grace is sufficient, and all things work together for good. We are promised eternal life through Jesus Christ. These are some of the promises from God, who is the creator of the heavens and the earth. Be assured that peace and love will stop murmuring and complaining dead in its tracks.

OBEDIENCE IN OUR LIVES

What does obedience in our lives represent to us? It assuredly means to persuade, to win over, to listen, to obey, to submit, and also to be under authority. Obedience also keeps us focused and determined to remain with our purpose to its conclusion. It keeps us from accepting worldly ways, and it strengthens and keeps us active and humble so that the light of Jesus can shine in and through us. Moreover, obedience in our lives keeps us attuned to the Holy Spirit, and as a result God can be glorified in all we put our hand to do.

When God made His promise to Abraham, there was no one greater for Him to swear by, and so He swore by Himself, saying to Abraham, "I will surely bless you and give you many descendants" (Heb. 6:14 NIV). Abraham was shown to us as the ultimate example of obedience: to wait no matter the problem, the solution, the circumstances, or how long it might possibly take for an answer. Without a doubt, know that being patient and obedient will eventually result in a great reward. Blessings will readily flow into your life when you clothe yourself continually in garments of joy, peace, patience, faithfulness, gentleness, goodness, kindness, and self-control (Gal. 5:22–23). Put on your outer wrap with lots of love, and add some obedience to complete your stylish new wardrobe.

OLYMPIC SPIRIT

An Olympic spirit allows you to have a vision, implement a plan, and fulfill it to your final goal. But first you should make a plan and implement it to the very last detail. This all comes to mind while watching athletes train and listening to their stories. Most had a seed that was planted in their childhood, and they never lost sight of the goal; some materialized theirs later in life. To compete and win, that's it in a nutshell—but there's more to it than those four words.

First, the athletes usually start with a training schedule that has to be strictly followed, no matter the weather or how they feel or what's going on around them. Second, they have a strict dietary schedule of knowing which foods to eat, which fluids to drink, and at what time for the maximum benefit for their body. Third, there has to be a rest schedule, how many hours of sleep are needed, what time to go to bed. Fourth, they welcome competition that will sharpen and hone their skills. When the day of the sporting event arrives, they will be available, equipped, ready, and filled up, knowing they have trained to the max "I can do all things through Christ which strengthens me" (Phil. 4:13 KJV). Steadily push on, and stay focused on the vision implanted in you to run the race of life and win with an Olympic spirit.

OPEN THE DOOR

Open the door. Whose door, what door, and why? Where is the door located? First, open the door of your life to a renewed attitude—to learning new things, experiencing new relationships, exploring new places, and maybe learning a new language.

Second, open the door to listen when others speak, witness when the opportunity presents itself, give when the need arises, and sometimes go out of your way to help others.

Third, open the door of your heart to love, trust, believe, and openly and willingly exhibit obedience. Fourth, open the door to the goodness of Jesus and tell someone what He has done in your life, how situations have changed, and how prayer really does change things if you stand on His Word.

Lastly, open the door to include the fruit of the Spirit, which is love, joy, peace, patience, kindness, goodness, faithfulness, gentleness, and self-control (Gal. 5:22–23a) and is always be evident in your life. "Set a guard, O Lord, over my mouth; Keep watch over the door of my lips. Do not incline my heart to any evil thing" (Ps. 141:3–4a NKJV). Open the door to read the Word daily, meditate on it, and let it resonate deep within you so that you can be an open door with hinges of faith that always swings outward for the benefit of others waiting for you.

OVERCOMING THE TRIALS OF LIFE

Trials and tribulations sometimes creep into your life without permission. When they do come, you may be so focused on the problem that you forget some of your past experiences and how you were able to overcome them. Perhaps you struggle to recall answers to prayers and the specific guidance provided to you by the Holy Spirit, or lessons learned in previous trials. Could it possibly be that your emotions inhibit clear, rational thinking? Nevertheless, go back through your journals and read what you wrote that helped you overcome whatever life situation you were facing. What did the Holy Spirit lead you to do? What prayers did you pray and which were answered? What did the Word speak to you as you read, listened to worship music, and sat quietly waiting for the Lord to speak?

If you have never overcome something, it's hard to imagine yourself being an overcomer. But was Jesus preparing His disciples for His departure and said, "These things I have spoken to you, that in me you may have peace. In the world you will have tribulation; but be of good cheer, I have overcome the world" (John 16:33 NKJV). Accept the reality of healing and wholeness, and be assured that you are more than an overcomer through Christ, who already has and will continue to strengthen, protect, and provide guidance for you to overcome whatever trials come into your life.

PEACE IN MY LIFE

Not having peace came from some stuff that slowly crept into my life without permission. I didn't recognize the fiery darts that got flung my way to discourage, sidetrack, or make me quit projects I was passionate about. I was reading my Bible, listening to praise and worship music, ministering to others, and praying for everything except being closer to Him. Having peace in my life came when I learned to let go of some things—well, most things—and let God have command of my life.

I recalled that it's not all about me, but about the "God who created the heavens and the earth" (Gen. 1:1). I was reminded that peace in my life rarely comes naturally. I have to constantly seek the peace *of* God, peace *with* God, and peace *from* God through prayer. Also, I have to ask for a daily infilling of God's peace, which passes all understanding. All of this is while I strive to grow to maturity the fruit of the Spirit, which is rooted inside of me. I am diligent about putting on my armor of God (Eph. 6:11) every morning before going out against the worldliness of life that might quietly envelope me without notice. "For the Kingdom of God is not eating and drinking, but righteousness and peace and joy in the Holy Spirit" (Rom. 14:17 NKJV). Let peace enter your life totally for all the positive results that surely will follow.

PEACE THAT PASSES ALL UNDERSTANDING

Peace is the freedom from disagreement, the end of a dispute or war, and perhaps the conclusion of an arduous task or journey. Peace is the absence of conflict, and it is being able to live without abuse, poverty, hunger, shame, harm, or danger. It is a state of mind obtained from letting go and letting God fill your inner space, and it's time to feed your inner man. Ultimately, it's the absence of worry and fatigue. "And the peace of God, which surpasses all understanding, will guard your hearts and minds through Christ Jesus" (Phil. 4:7 NKJV). The peace that passes all understanding comes when the manifestation of the Spiritual fruit cultivated within us and nourishes us to health and wholeness.

But sometimes peace is fleeting because we allow worldly influences and attitudes to slowly or unknowingly creep into our lives. Without a doubt, peace rarely comes naturally. We have to constantly seek the peace *of* God, peace *with* God, and peace *from* God through prayer, praise, and worship. Be blessed in your quiet time, and ask to be filled with the peace that passes all understanding. Know that Jesus is the prince of peace and that we have been given the authority to be peacemakers. Readily let peace transcend over into all aspects of your life, and let the blessings flow outward.

Prayer Life Reflections

When you pray, do you have a special time and place to pray? Are you specific in your prayer requests, and do you spend enough time in prayer? Do you always ask instead of thanking God for His goodness, mercy, and grace in your life? Are you willing to wait for an answer to your prayer, and are you obedient to follow where He guides you in His answer, whatever it may be? Do you consider that it is a privilege we have when we go to God in prayer? Do you approach prayer in boldness and confidence for favorable results that line up with the promises of God?

As you examine yourself and mature in the Word, you will be able to remain in a sincere relationship with God in everything you do and all through your prayer life as well. "If my people who are called by my name, will humble themselves and pray and seek my face and turn from their wicked ways then will I hear from heaven and will forgive their sin and will heal their land" (2 Chron. 7:14 NIV). Be blessed as you reflect on strengthening and maturing your prayer life for grace, wisdom, and discernment in order to influence others to do the same for the greater good of the kingdom yet to come.

Pressing on but Still Fearful

You're pressing on but still fearful, because your situation hasn't come to a solid conclusion. Could it be the loss of a job, and you have to move due to a mortgage foreclosure? Is it the result of an accident, illness, divorce, or death of a loved one? All these situations will lead you to think about what the future will hold. Pressing on but still fearful in some situations might be a little frustrating, like not being able to write or spell well, or the fear of speaking in front of a large audience. Could it be the loss of your identity or self-respect, the loss of vision for your purpose in life, or perhaps a momentary lapse of memory?

Sometimes anger and bitterness can overwhelm you to a point that life itself will make it seem like you are going to lose your mind, and then you really won't be able to deal with any loss in your life. But remember—"And my God shall supply every need of yours according to His riches in glory in Christ Jesus" (Phil. 4:19 ASV). Minimize your losses by being proactive in and with your own life, so that when a "pressing on but still fearful" situation arises, you will be able to overcome it with a new outlook and a new attitude for positive, lifelong results.

READING IS THE KEY TO LIFE

One of the greatest joys of life is being able to read and have some comprehension of what you have read. Some people read to learn in school via textbooks, some seek to gain insight into different aspects of life, some read for pleasure or leisure to stave off boredom, and some read self-help books for improvement. Some read the Word for guidance and wisdom that the Holy Spirit reveals to them. "For the Lord gives wisdom; from his mouth comes knowledge and understanding" (Prov. 2:6 NKJV). Have you ever considered reading aloud to someone who is sick, shut-in, or blind? Perhaps you can tutor someone in a math, science or music class, whichever is your expertise?

Why not start a new tradition and set an example by reading along with your children? Observe the joy and wonder of someone who has never held a book in their hands or had the opportunity to know the joy of some of the treasures that are revealed in reading a book. Whatever your concept of reading is, it's a key that will unlock the wonders of the world, and it will allow you to enjoy one of the greatest freedoms you have in this country: being able to read without censorship.

Remember Who You Are

Why do we have to remember who we are? Won't we be the same as we were yesterday, today, and tomorrow? Maybe, but remembering ensures pride, envy, anger, rudeness, and unforgiveness don't take root in your heart, ruling and perhaps ruining your life. Remember who you are so that someone else doesn't define your character, set the parameters on your talent, limit your education, and thwart your ambitions. Focus on the positives in your life in order to make a difference, and sow some seeds in someone's life practices for a positive change. Remember who you are so that you can affect change for the homeless, the helpless, and those living in the shadows of civilization.

Take some time to reminisce and remember who you really are. You are definitely capable of being mature, giving, serving, and loving in all aspects of what you were purposed to do in God's kingdom. "Remember me, O Lord with the favor you have toward your people" (Ps. 106:4 NKJV). Hark back to who you are as you take a trip down memory lane. Ascertain what caused you to grow into the person you are today. Reflect back on how far you've come in life and who you used to be, and acknowledge the person you have become today.

REWARDS

Have you encountered all the reward options you can get just for filling out a piece of paper at various places of business—at the bank, the gasoline station, online, or via offers through the mail? It seems that everywhere you go, they have a rewards plan. Some of them are free, and some require a small fee. Some plans do give a quarterly cash dividend or a future discount off on merchandise. Some banks will add up the points for trips, rental cars, or other merchandise. I have a wallet full of rewards cards to more places than I care to reveal. The question is, why don't merchants lower their prices or upgrade their merchandise? As customers, are we so consumer savvy that we have to be enticed into their places of business with the promise of some type of reward? It seems to me that we are encouraged to acquire more stuff and store up our treasures on earth. "For where your treasure is there your heart will be also" (Luke 12:34 NKJV).

Your real rewards will come later, free of cost and with acquired benefits, like buying a bag of groceries for a family in need. Why not get a prescription filled for a senior citizen, and you pay for it? Give a caregiver the day off to get a pedicure and a manicure, or pay for a day at the spa for a friend. These are rewards that don't require a card to purchase, and there's no expiration date on them. Some rewards simply come from a heart filled with love.

RESOLUTIONS

The definition of a resolution is determining, resolving, or deciding to do something with future action or goals in mind. But resolutions have to be doable so that they won't be so hard to obtain. Write your goals down so you can keep track of your progress; write in your journal your feelings about starting a new regimen or a life-altering route. Sometimes resolutions or promises are about what's inside that needs to come to the outside. A new life plan for your resolutions could be eating less and moving more, complaining less and praying more, spending less and giving more, or driving less and walking more.

Whatever is your "less or more" add up to, it should be a realistic endeavor that can be obtained with satisfactory end results. It takes at least twenty-one days to break and create habits, so don't beat yourself up if one of the wheels fall off your resolution wagon, and you eat or do something you resolved not to do. Write in your food journal and observe how other people handle situations without getting thrown off course. Lower your expectations into manageable increments if they're too high. Paul wrote, "I press on toward the goal to win the prize for which God has called me heavenward in Christ Jesus" (Phil. 3:14 NIV). Above all else, keep striving forward and don't quit, because seeking out a new you with your new resolutions will soon become a comfortable part of your everyday life journey.

SEARCH FOR SIGNIFICANCE

Humankind has been on a search for its significance since time began. Our significance often relates to our importance, being noticed, being secure, having a measure of personal success, status and beauty, a fair amount of wealth, and the approval of others. Our inner longing is to be healthy, wealthy, and wise and to have love and to be loved. Our outer reality is to be gracious, polite, trustworthy, thoughtful, caring, benevolent, understanding, patient, and slow to anger. Our self-esteem or significance is usually a reflection of our surroundings: our upbringing in a loving environment, the attitudes of our siblings, our neighborhood, and schools attended play a huge part in our lives. Oftentimes the search for our significance culminates in our restlessness, and that has a lot to do with our anger, unforgiveness, broken communications and relationships, and indifference to people around us (who perhaps sensed a prideful attitude).

Could it be you always want to be right and talk over people in a discussion, to show how much you know? That sounds like a search for significance to me. Perhaps you want to show your importance! "Search me, O God, and know my heart: try me and know my thoughts" (Ps. 139:23 KJV). The key to the betterment of life should begin with a new you who has arrived and is no longer on an improbable quest to find out who you are and where you fit into the total scheme of the world.

SECOND CHANCE

Reflect for a moment on what a second chance means to you. It's an opportunity to redo something that wasn't quite right the first time. Maybe a second chance came after recovery from an illness, accident, or surgery, or there's a reconciliation of a marriage to renew a long-forgotten friendship. Perhaps a second chance came on a job or school assignment. Think about all the people we read about in the Bible who were given second chances. Moses was called by God to lead the Israelites out of Egypt. David repented, asked for God's forgiveness, and was anointed king over Israel. Job was restored after he had been faithfully tested. The woman with the issue of blood touched the hem of Jesus's garment. Lazarus was raised from the dead by Jesus. On the road to Damascus, Paul was chosen to take the gospel to the Gentiles. God restored Jesus back to glory unto Himself.

Consider changes with your second chances. Eat less and move more, call a relative just to say hello and catch up on life, send a card, invite someone to a meal, get involved in an outreach program, love yourself more, do some act of kindness that nobody knows about except you and the Lord, and definitely tell someone about the One who gives second chances unconditionally just because He loves you. "Many are the afflictions of the righteous; but the Lord delivers him out of them all" (Ps. 34:19 NKJV). Be an encouragement to others as you live your life to the fullest, and be grateful for each day as a gift of a second chance, and count all of your many blessings.

SEEKING AND LONGING FOR GOD

To seek means to diligently search for, aim at, attempt to find, or relentlessly pursue an object or action. Seeking often requires brokenness and pain as you encounter and uncover old hurts, unmet promises, expectations, and unfulfilled goals. It causes you to pull away from the crowd and do what is not proper or popular. Perhaps you have to let go of your dependency on other people, your family and friends, and go it alone. Be assured that you won't be alone. "And ye shall seek me, and find me, when ye shall search for me with all your heart" (Jer. 29:13 KJV).

Ultimately, you may finally realize that you're seeking and longing for God's presence and His establishment in every area of your life. The empty spaces and unfulfilled aspirations in your life cannot be fulfilled without the unconditional love of God. It is absolutely paramount that your character be shaped and strengthened by your bonded relationship with Him on the path of life until eternity. Be blessed as you go through life growing, maturing, and maintaining a meaningful and loving relationship with your family, friends, coworkers, and neighbors. Realistically love others despite all that has transpired in your life as you seek and long for God's everlasting assurance, love, and faithfulness.

SMILES

Smiles are a facial expression that usually show affection, agreement, amusement, approval, friendliness, or genuine pleasure. Smiles denote a healthy and happy attitude that translates into longevity and a fruit-producing lifestyle. Friendships, relationships, some business dealings, and commitments are sealed with a signature on the last line, a handshake, maybe a hug, and definitely a smile. Staunch attitudes and harsh words are turned around with a smile. Sometimes people bring sunshine to cloudy days with a smile at the right time; others bring a calmness to chaos with a smile. Some leave their legacies and imprints on our hearts and in our lives by the joy that flows forth and begins with a smile.

Realistically, how many of us are pleased and smile at the events that happen in our lives? Sometime our spouses, children, jobs, or neighbors don't warrant a smile, but make it a practice to smile and be happy anyway. Observe a change in the environment and the situations around from just a smile. Smile and wave at the person in the car next to you in rush hour traffic. Smile at the cashier after waiting in line a long time. Smile and realize how good God has been to you. Miraculously, even when God rested after seven days of Creation, (Genesis 2:1-3 NIV) I'm sure He was all smiles and enjoyed all his completed handiwork.

So Many Things to
Be Thankful For

There are so many things to be thankful for. A mess to clean up after a party, because it means you were surrounded with friends. The taxes you pay means you are employed, and the clothes that fit a little too snug means you have more than enough to eat. What about all the complaining about the government and its policies? It simply means you have freedom of speech in this country.

Be thankful for a lawn that needs mowing, windows that need cleaning, and gutters that need fixing, because it means you have a home. Be thankful for the piles of laundry to sort and wash; most likely it means your loved ones are nearby. Realize that you have so many things to be thankful for. The lady behind you sings off-key, and it means you can hear and she can still use her voice. When you park at the far end of the lot, it means you are still mobile; the shadow that follows you about means you are outside and enjoying the sunshine.

"Enter his gates with thanksgiving, and into His courts with praise. Be thankful to Him, and bless His name" (Ps. 100:4 NKJV). Remember that there are so many things to be thankful for: humility instead of pride, generosity instead of covetousness, restraint instead of lust and wickedness, kindness instead of anger, moderation instead of gluttony, diligence instead of carelessness, and lots of love over hatred, anger, and worldliness.

STANDARDS OF QUALITY
AND VIRTUE

Consider some of your standards of quality and virtue in your daily activities. They probably should include some humility, to know that you are not alone in a world of supplementary opinions. There's the virtue of generosity, to permit others to have what they deserve, and some restraint to control your most passionate impulses. The quality of kindness is to tolerate the mistakes of others and not jump to conclusions about their outcomes. The virtue of trust is to believe that everything will work according to your proposed plan of life. The virtue of moderation is to satisfy yourself with the necessities of life. The virtue of charity is to willingly help those who are unable to help themselves. The quality of diligence is to make yourself useful in the world no matter the place, race, or culture.

All of these traits are seen not through the eyes, but through your interpretations, your perceptions, and your understanding. "I have fought a good fight, I have finished my course, I have kept the faith" (2 Tim. 4:7 KJV). In the manner indicated above, incorporate some of these standards of quality and virtues into the corners of your life. Consequently, know without a doubt that you are highly favored and truly loved because of your honest, faithful, and loving attitude to always do the right thing with your excellent standards of quality and virtues in your life.

STRESS IN THE WORLD

Nowadays there are lots of stressors in the world. Every day some traumatic, dangerous, and life-altering event is happening somewhere in the world. We now have instant access to news as it happens, but does it benefit us to be tuned into drama twenty-four seven? Bomb threats, mass shootings, plane crashes, automobile recalls due to faulty workmanship, ongoing wars, famines, and extreme weather. Some folks act crazy for the sake of making the latest newscast.

There seems to be an increase of stress in the world, but don't allow your life to be invaded, bombarded, or taken over by the negativity of what is happening. You have the right to excuse yourself from the six o'clock newscast, and to go to bed worry free at eleven without allowing the stress in the world to replay in your mind all night long. Read the Word before going to bed, dim the bedroom lights, play some soft music, pray, mediate, and be thankful for the goodness in your life. "The Lord is my strength and my shield; my heart trusted in Him, and I am helped: therefore my heart greatly rejoices, and with my song I will praise Him" (Ps. 28:7 NKJV). Be assured that you are more than a conqueror of stress in the world. Make sure you are safe, sane, and saved from the mayhem, and enjoy your life to the fullest.

STORMS IN LIFE

What is a storm? It's a strong outburst of emotion or anger, a disturbance or upheaval of a political or social nature, a sneak attack on a fortified place, or an atmospheric disturbance. All of these definitions signify storms in life—situations that are out of the ordinary order of the day. They sweep through our lives, and some are beyond our control. There are storms of finance (having more month than money) and storms of relationships (dealing with anger and disappointment). Storms of education involve no career opportunities in sight and mounting student loan debt to pay. The storms of health include diabetes, arthritis, high cholesterol, and perhaps no health coverage.

But keep pushing on, because storms in life don't last forever. Make sure you store up provisions, food, water, and batteries. Keep checking on job prospects, stay healthy by eating right, and get enough sleep so that when opportunities do present themselves—and eventually they will—you'll be ready, available, and equipped. "And there will be a tabernacle for shade in the daytime from the heat, for a place of refuge, and for a shelter from storm and rain" (Isa. 4:6 NKJV). Be blessed going through the storms of life that will produce strength, courage, determination, integrity, a new attitude, and a measurable amount of joy. Be thoroughly prepared for the sun to shine after the storms in life pass, when a rainbow appears in the sky and the sun shines brightly.

STRENGTHENING YOUR HEART

The heart is the strongest, most essential muscle in the human body. Sometimes hearts are happy and glad, some are empty and sad, some are regretful and remorseful, and perhaps some are still angry, lonely, and unloved. Whatever your state of being, hearts can be changed into more useful, positive, life-giving vessels. *First,* begin to focus on the positive aspects of your life; be thankful and grateful for who you are and what you already have. *Second,* focus on God, who created the heavens and the earth, and praise Him for life itself. *Third,* pray for others as well as yourself that situations will be forgiven, healed, redeemed, and reconciled. Have faith that change will transpire in God's time, and make time to read and believe His promises in the Word. *Fourth,* encourage yourself and others to remain empty in order to be renewed, refilled, and refreshed with the fruit of the Spirit (Gal. 5:22–23), and to be dressed daily in the armor of God (Eph. 6:10–18).

As you exercise and strengthen your heart to "Above all else, guard your heart, for it is the wellspring of life" (Prov. 4:23 NIV), prepare yourself to receive new mercies every day. Actively exercise to strengthen your heart through reading the Word and through worship, prayer, and praise. When you have reinforced your body, mind, and soul, a new outlook will also follow.

TAKE CARE OF YOURSELF

What does it mean to take care of yourself, and in what context? Does it mean to look your best, with hair combed, teeth brushed, and clothes neat? Taking care of you means not only on the outside but on the inside as well. Do you eat food that is nourishing? Do you read and play word games in order to stimulate your brain and keep your mind stretched? Do you walk or exercise at least three times a week to keep your body healthy and your joints limber? Do you pray and read the Word to keep your spirit alive? Do you nourish relationships with your family, neighbors, coworkers, and church folks? Do you cherish your time spent with your spouse or children? How about your own hobbies or activities? Do you contribute your time, talent, or treasure to make a difference and sow seeds for change?

Remember you have twenty-four hours in every day, and how you spend them is up to you. "I will praise you, for I am fearfully and wonderfully made; Marvelous are your works" (Ps. 139:14b NKJV). In view of your daily activities, be sure to take care of yourself as you encounter the speed bumps in life. You were made for a purpose designed only for you, and you should always be ready to take care of yourself so you can run the race of life and finish well, to be used in the kingdom of life.

THE OUTWARD DISCIPLINES OF LIFE

What are the character of the outward disciplines or attributes that should be a part of our daily makeup to produce a lifestyle that brings satisfaction and stability into our lives? Simplicity is a liberating act of release that freely detaches us from whatever possessions we have so that we can genuinely enjoy them without a covetous concern for them. Solitude is an attitude of aloneness and silence in a place of quiet inner peace—a place where, when God speaks to us, we are able to hear Him. The act of submission frees us and makes it possible to distinguish between genuine situations and our obstinate self-will as we learn to value other people and love them unconditionally because it is our Christian obligation to do so. Our service to others is provided simply and given faithfully, and there is no need to calculate the results.

The grace of humility, patience, and perseverance are outward disciplines of life that are slowly infused into our lives, with a sense of inner satisfaction that fills us for the journey of our lifetime. What we do daily becomes a part of who we are. "Therefore humble yourselves under the mighty hand of God, that he may exalt you in due time" (1 Pet. 5:6 NKJV). Be free from worry as you develop your outward character disciplines, put them into practice at every opportunity that you encounter, and enlighten someone along the pathway of life.

THE SPRING CLEANING RITUAL

Spring cleaning: the annual ritual that may remind you of drudgery and hard work without an end. Nevertheless, it is an opportunity to rid your environment of all the unused, unwanted stuff. Spring cleaning is not just about cleaning your house, car, garage, or yard, but cleaning the clutter out of your mind, your heart, your spirit, your mouth, and your life.

Imagine a clutter-free environment where you can breathe and entertain some sane thoughts, as well as have an opportunity to reevaluate your life, health, exercise regime, eating habits, and family or career goals. After all the clutter in your life has been separated, sifted, reorganized, or disbursed, then when your heavenly father speaks, you'll be able to hear and respond to Him through prayer, praise, and worship. Remember—"But lay up for yourselves treasures in heaven, where neither moth nor rust doth corrupt, and where thieves do not break through nor steal; For where your treasure is, there your heart will be also" (Matt. 6:20–21 KJV). In a clutter-free environment, you should be more relaxed and motivated to focus on your purpose and direction in life. Thankfully, you'll be free to respond with clearer understanding and compassion. Then perhaps you'll realize that the spring cleaning ritual is necessary to produce endless life benefits.

THE PURPOSE OF SIGNS

Ponder for a moment the purpose of signs, what they mean, and the purpose for which we use them. A sign could be a gesture or motion that conveys information, a command, or an indication of an upcoming event. It could point the way as in a direction or be a mark or symbol. Could people be waiting and wanting to see a sign so they can gauge their remaining time to be wicked and perverse as they inch toward the Day of Judgment? Sexual immorality, selfish ambition, greed, drunkenness, entitlement, bigotry, unforgiveness, political unrest, and racial hatred have almost become the norm for this generation. The Pharisees told Jesus, "We want to see a sign from you, and Jesus answered, a wicked and adulterous generation seeks after a sign" (Matt. 12:38b–39a NKJV).

We as believers are the sign people are looking for, as displayed through our joy, peace, patience, kindness, gentleness, goodness, faithfulness, gentleness, and self-control (Gal. 5:22–23 KJV), which are all wrapped in love. We have been given all power and authority here on earth over the rulers of wickedness, if we realize how to use them for the betterment of all peoples regardless of race, culture, color, or circumstances. We must realize that we are the signs that point the way.

TRIALS AND TRIBULATIONS

There are lots of activities going on in the world, both good and bad. Aren't you glad to know whose side you're on and the team that is supporting and cheering you on to victory? It is written in the Bible that we have a great cloud of witnesses as examples of faith that sustained them in their darkest times of trouble (Heb. 11:1–40). We should be encouraged by our trials and tribulations, because how else would we know that God can and will answer our prayers? How would we learn that He is our provider and protector, and where He leads, He always provides. How would we know our strength comes from Him? How would we know the joy that comes in the morning after a night of doubt, worry, and anguish? "Trust in the Lord with all thine heart; and lean not unto thine own understanding" (Prov. 3:5 KJV). And how would we know to trust the Holy Spirit who lives in us?

As you go along the pathway of life, you should pick up some wisdom, strength, joy, and peace, which will culminate in a fantastic sense of accomplishment that you have become an overcomer in how to handle the trials and tribulations of life.

Thankful and Blessed

What circumstances, situations, or events have happened in your life that have caused you to be thankful and blessed? First, the wondrous workings of the human body: a brain with saneness of mind, clarity of eyesight, fullness of hearing, touch sensations, different emotions, the ability to freely move about, the ability to taste and eat and use the nutrients for their intended purpose, and the rejuvenation from peaceful sleep. You have freedom to speak, move about, and live wherever you can afford, obtain a higher education, and seek a career of your choosing.

Most of all, you should be thankful and blessed you have the freedom to openly worship, own a Bible, and be able to read the Word whenever and wherever you want. "O Lord of hosts, blessed is the man that trusts in you" (Ps. 84:12 KJV). Be thankful and blessed for God's Son, who lives in your spirit, allows the fruit of the Spirit to grow within you, and gives you the assurance of victory with eternal salvation. Joyfully go about being thankful and realize how blessed you are. Have a smile on your face, a song on your lips, and abundant joy in your heart for life itself.

THE IMPORTANCE OF YOUR ADDRESS

An address could be a written or spoken speech, a dwelling, a place to send or receive a message, and a place to receive packages or other correspondence. Is your address located in one of the most prestigious gated communities in a city, in an influential part of town? Is it in the right school district, or where the better stores are located with good prices and availability of food? Is your address in a safe part of town with no police sirens, no helicopters overhead, and no drive-bys? Do you think that the wilderness of the world will contaminate the garden of your spirit if left abandoned and unattended?

You might ask, "Whose spirit?" Ours, of course! We should be encouraged with how our actions ought to unfold in our surrounding circumstances, and we should look for ways to improve and address our actions. "For wherever you go I will go; and wherever you lodge, I will lodge; your people shall be my people, and your God, my God" (Ruth 1:16b NKJV). You have the power to change the spiritual, mental, emotional, and physical addresses of your life. Your salvation from darkness to light enables you to be a transfer agent for yourself and others to change addresses if deemed necessary. Enjoy the privilege and power of a life free of strife by the changes that can occur in your life when you adjust to a new address.

TRAINING FOR THE LONG HAUL

In my neighborhood, the joggers are out early and in full force, training for various marathons. They have to run and endure the race to the end, in any kind of weather and on any terrain. Men and women of all ages and stages are running in groups throughout the community. They know that endurance, strength, stamina, and preparation will allow them to compete and possibly win a grueling 26.2-mile race. Not everyone will win, but knowing the preparation and "stick to it" attitude that was necessary to compete is enough for some to be overjoyed about their accomplishment. How many of us know without a doubt that we want to be successful and win at whatever our life goal is? It takes a mind, spirit, and body all working in unison to succeed.

Paul writes, "Do you not know that those who run in a race all run, but one receives the prize? Run in such a way that you may obtain it" (1 Cor. 9:24 NKJV). Absolutely be blessed as you train for the purpose in your life and the calling on your life. Be thankful for strength, good health, belief in yourself, and the obedience to stick to your training regimen. Trust that it will work out all right. Moreover, encourage someone to train with your jogging team or just for exercise, so that they'll be mentally and physically able to have endurance for the long-haul race of life experiences yet to come.

THE CHOICE IS YOURS

The choice is yours in a lot of different aspects of daily life. You can speak out against bullying, whether in school, at work, or in church. The choice is yours to walk away from smoking, drugs, and underage sexual experiences. Perhaps it's your choice to show yourself as friendly in order to make friends. Help to feed the hungry, provide shelter for the homeless, and offer support for the hopeless. It is a personal choice, and only you can decide to participate. It is definitely your choice to forgive, love, be happy, and give yourself away so that you can be used to make the world a better place. Choose to sow seeds for change in order to make a difference in life, and let your light shine in the darkness.

Every day we have a mound of choices to make—physical, mental, financial, and social. Have good judgment in what you decide, and make it permanent. God spoke to the prophet, and the choice is yours to believe that "I have chosen the way of truth; your judgments I have laid before me" (Ps. 119:30 NKJV). The choice to put some goodness first on your to-do list and then freely give it away. Take some positive action and spread some loving kindness, peace, joy, and happiness to everyone you meet with a friendly smile.

THE HEART OF A SERVANT

A servant is someone who performs duties for another. Servants meet the needs or satisfy requirements, and they assist wherever or whenever needed. But what does the heart of a servant look and perform like? *First,* the heart of a servant is emptied of pride and envy so he can focus on the situation without bias. *Second,* he is willing to be obedient and follow instructions no matter the circumstances or outcome. *Third,* he gives unconditionally and does not expect a reward or compensation for his services. *Fourth,* his gifts will be developed and used for his intended purpose of servitude. Moreover, the heart of a servant is giving and sharing, doing for others in order to make a difference in his family, community, school system, and place of worship as he shows humility, compassion, and love. "If any man serve me, let him follow me; and where I am, there shall also my servant be, if any man serve me, him will my Father honor" (John 12:26 KJV).

Intentionally sow some seeds for change in order to make a difference. Serve with the heart of a servant, along with commitment, obedience, and responsibility. Above all, serve without any reservations of your time, talent, and treasure, with lots of love and with honor and reverence to God.

TAKING THE FIRST STEP

Just what does taking the first step look like? After planning and much preparation, you step out into a new career, or you decide to get married instead of simply living together. Perhaps it's time to move to another home in another city. What if you are taking the first step to speak out against an unjust practice in your workplace, or a pattern of discrimination against the poor, homeless, or helpless who have no voice to be heard? Evil prevails and spreads when good people do nothing, and yet we wonder why nothing has changed.

When taking the first step, don't be afraid to unlock the door of prejudice, harassment, or bullying. The world needs more people who are taking the first step to move things along, out of the rut of life, and onto the straight path to victory. You might be all alone in your quest for change, but know that you should "Withhold no good from them to whom it is due, when it is in the power of thine hand to do it" (Prov. 3:27 KJV). As you're taking the first step, watch for others who might join you in the pursuit of a situation that needs to be addressed, remedied, or dissolved for the betterment of all concerned.

THE DESIRES OF YOUR HEART

What are the desires of your heart, and how do you achieve them? A desire is something you wish for, crave for, or covet. Perhaps you have a deep longing for something. It is a feeling or an idea that is inside you until it is acted upon. Is one of your desires of your heart to be rich and famous, to be beautiful and trim, to be well liked with lots of friends, to be well educated, or to live free from the everyday cares of life? The desires of your heart will come when you give yourself away so that you can be used for service, while emptying yourself of anger, pride, unforgiveness, and selfishness. "Therefore my heart rejoiced, and my tongue was glad; moreover my flesh also will rest in hope" (Acts 2:26 NKJV).

However, ask yourself whether the desires of your heart are in line with making a difference in the world while sowing seeds for change. Those actions should be the primary desire of your heart, and then all other actions will follow. Watch the blessings multiply in your life as you trust, obey, commit, and implement all the desires of your heart for a more enriched and balanced lifestyle.

THANKFUL FOR ALL
THAT YOU HAVE

Being thankful for all that you have encompasses having the activity of your limbs, saneness of mind, your eyesight, and your hearing. It involves the ability to clearly speak, to smell, to taste, to touch, to breathe, to laugh, to interact with people, and to have emotions. Above all else, be thankful that you have the freedom to move about from your home, job, neighborhood, city, state, and country. Be thankful that you have freedom to worship at the church of your choice, and that you can praise, pray, and read the Word without persecution. Be thankful for all that you have encompasses having the sun, which God allows to shine, warm the earth, and make things grow. The sun provides you with energy, light, and vitamins A and D.

You also have the Son, who radiates in your spirit, allows the fruit of the Spirit to grow within you (Gal. 5:22–23), gives you the assurance of victory, and gives you eternal life. "Therefore I say to you, do not worry about your life, what you will eat; nor about the body, what you will put on. Life is more than food, and the body is more than clothing" (Luke 12:22–23 NKJV). Be thankful and tell someone about the goodness of life itself and what it means to you, as well as the abundant love of God mixed with grace and mercy added to your life.

THE RIGHT TIME

Think for a moment about time—some time, daytime, nighttime, or any time. We speak about time as something that just exists, as if it's always there. But what does it mean to you to know when it is the right time? Or is it ever the right time? The right time might be when you don't put off an assignment that is due, or making a phone call to a relative. It could be asking someone you offended for forgiveness so that you can get on with your life. Could the right time be loving and giving more, and murmuring and complaining less? Those are probably the right times.

If necessary, the right time is when you speak out about an issue that involves your city, your neighborhood, your church, or some compromised morality issue that is disturbing to young people. You'll know without a doubt when it is the right time, because it feels good when you speak up or get involved. You feel a sense of relief, and joy is exhibited when you have made a difference and sowed some seeds for change. "Now may the God of patience and comfort grant you to be like-minded toward one another according to Christ Jesus" (Rom. 15:5 NKJV). As you boldly speak out with discretion and get involved to do the right, be blessed to know the right time that everything that has been purposed to you will be accomplished with joy, integrity, honesty, and lots of love.

TELLING YOUR STORY

Telling your story involves the experiences in your life that brought you through adversities or sorrows, and you are still sane and sober. Telling your story might help someone overcome an addiction to drugs, alcohol, food, or some other inappropriate behavior. It could possibly free people from an abusive relationship or a physical infirmary that saps their strength, drains their mental energy, or robs them of their peace of mind. Upon hearing your story, they might think if you made it over and through, then perhaps they can too.

Believe it or not, people want to know that their problems are not unique to them, that somebody else went through a similar situation and survived to become a different person. "Listen, for I will speak of excellent things, and from the opening of my lips will come right things" (Prov. 8:6 NKJV). When you are telling your story, you are freeing others from bondage, helping them possibly to see a way out of a dangerous or an unpleasant situation and into a new attitude about life and loving themselves. So speak up and strive to make a difference by telling your story, even if you do not think what you say counts. It really does matter to someone who needs confirmation.

THE PRIVILEGE OF PRAYER

Having the privilege of prayer allows you to be free and able to pray anytime, anywhere, and in any environment or circumstance. Do you make take time to pray? Are you specific in your prayer requests? Are you willing to wait for an answer to your prayers? Are you obedient to follow where He guides you in His answer? Have you ever considered that the privilege of prayer is granted because of God's love for you? Sometime the answers to prayers are yes, no, wait, or not at all. Does that mean you stop praying? No. It is written, "If my people who are called by my name, will humble themselves and pray and seek my face and turn from their wicked ways, then I will hear from heaven and will forgive their sin and heal their land" (2 Chron. 7:14 NKJV).

As you examine yourself and mature in the Word, you will be able to sustain and remain throughout your prayer life in a sincere relationship with God. Prayer seems to be just what we need at this time, with the pervasive evil of discontent enveloping the land. We need to remember that God is always on time, and in His time (not ours) He answers our prayers. So be blessed in your prayer life filled with joy, love, and peace for whatever the outcome to your prayers may be, now or later.

THANKFUL FOR A FULL LIFE

Why not start your day off being thankful for a full life—your saneness of mind, the activity of your limbs, peace when you lay down to sleep, nourishment when you get hungry, monetary funds to buy food and pay bills, a running automobile with gas in the tank, and love of family and close friends? Most of all, be thankful for your relationship with God, your confessed assurance of salvation, your uplifting praise and worship, and your evangelism and sharing the good news of the Gospel. A full life of thanks is because you have lived long enough for your hair to turn grey, and lines are etched deep in your face from worry and laughter. Some folks have died before experiencing the joys of aging, bulging bellies, sagging breasts, or swaying hips. As you grow older, it is easier to be positive and care less about what people think, and to not question yourself so much anymore; besides, you have earned the right to sometimes be wrong! "Thanks be to God for his indescribable gift" (2 Cor. 9:15 NIV). In view of your appreciation and gratitude, it is better to have relationships in your life and be thankful that they will provide balance, support, teachable moments, and correction if needed.

UNDER THE INFLUENCE

Are you under the influence? I don't mean drinking, drugs, or some other vice, but the influence of the Holy Spirit. Has the fruit of the Spirit (Gal. 5:22–23) been made manifest in your life? Are you under the influence of God's love, with a desire to please Him, do good for mankind, and give energy to faith itself? How about joy, the rejoicing that arises from a sense of God's mercy communicated to the soul in the pardon of sin with the prospect of eternal life. Maybe you have peace, the calm and quiet serenity that floods our justified souls as a result of our reconciliation with God. Long-suffering is bearing the frailties and provocations of others through a myriad of difficulties, without murmuring or complaining. Kindness is concern for others, with a desire to treat them as God treats us. Goodness is a moral and spiritual excellence manifested by positive action on our part. Faithfulness is a person who can be trusted and is loyal and truthful in their word and promises. Meekness is based on humility, total submission, being teachable, and being considerate of others. Self-control helps us restrain our human passions and appetites, and display an attitude that is pleasing to God. "For in him we live and move and have our being" (Acts 17:28 NKJV). Moreover, being under the influence of the Holy Spirit allows us to be grounded in the pursuit of our purpose and calling, also cultivated to have an abundance of the fruit of the Spirit in the garden of our lives forever.

UNCONDITIONAL LOVE

The world operates on conditional love, but God operates on His divine, unconditional love for us. We don't have to do anything to earn it, and it can't be bought. Many people believe that working hard will produce love, and often they seek it in inappropriate places, people, and things. God gave His only Son to pay the price for our salvation after we sinned, and His Son died willingly on the cross. Now, that's unconditional love! "While we were yet sinners, Christ died for us" (Rom. 5:8b KJV).

No matter what has happened in your past or what's happening in your life right now, you will always have the unconditional love of God. But how are you giving unconditional love to others? You might start with dying to self for a renewed lifestyle. It could be forgiving someone or yourself, or forgetting something that happened long ago that will finally release you from anger, pain, and bitterness. Donate some blankets, or slightly worn clothes to a homeless shelter, volunteer at a soup kitchen, encourage persons who have lost hope with prayer and direct them to resources for a better way of life, or maybe clean house for a senior citizen. These are all what constitute quality of life episodes of unconditional love, and most likely they're of little cost to the giver. Ask yourself. "What am I doing to give some unconditional love away and to make a difference in someone's life today?"

WATCH YOUR WORDS

Watch your words, because they have meaning and are used to convey deep feelings, beliefs, and ideas. Watch your words so that anger, hatred, bitterness, betrayal, pride, and unforgiveness don't wound or affect another person's self-worth for a lifetime. Words spoken without thought, in anger, or as a rebuke to people can cut like a knife through their existence, and it may leave permanent scars on their inner being. Words are powerful, and once spoken they cannot be reclaimed; they are not easily forgotten or forgiven. Consider that words have meaning that build up or tear down. Express love, happiness, and joy. Words can instruct, rebuke, or correct, but they can also reconcile and rejoice.

In essence, words can be used to speak peace for safety and sanity. When spoken in prayer, they can bring about a change in the atmosphere. But be careful to realize that words spoken in different cultures have different meanings, and some words evolve differently over time. "So then, my beloved brethren, let every man be swift to hear, slow to speak, slow to wrath; for the wrath of man does not produce the righteousness of God" (James 1:19–20 NKJV). Be careful as you choose your words wisely for the greatest understanding, impact, and clarity. Above all else, be mindful of your tone.

WHAT FREE WILL MEANS TO US

We have certain freedoms from the control and influence of others over our lives. But those rights and privileges are based on ideas from man. Emotional and mental freedoms cannot be written and listed on a piece of paper. Consider life experiences that control and influence the circumstances that produce the freedom of *not* being locked up in jail, of *not* being sick or incapacitated in a hospital bed. However, consider the freedom that allows you to travel anywhere; eat what you want and when you want; live where you want, purchase anything your money can buy; attend the school of your choice for higher learning; overcome cultural, class, and color challenges; and make a myriad of choices during each day.

Furthermore, those freedoms are minute compared to the One who gives eternal life, the freedom to worship when and where you choose, the freedom to have and openly read a Bible, and the freedom to forgive and love as God demonstrated for us through His son. "God so loved the world" (John 3:16 NIV). Moreover, be grateful and enjoy all the freedoms that you now have, and please don't take them for granted. "Accept, I pray the freewill offerings of my mouth, O Lord, and teach me your judgments" (Ps. 119:108 NKJV).

WHY ARE WE HERE?

Take a moment to ponder why we were born, why we are here, and what is our purpose. We're not here by accident; God spoke clearly to the prophet Jeremiah, "Before I formed you in the womb I knew you, before you were born I sanctified you, I ordained you as a prophet to the nations" (Jer. 1:5 NKJV). We're here on assignment to praise and worship God, because God inhabits the praises of His people. We are saved to seek Him in everything we do to, for His glory. We are here to walk by faith and not by sight while keeping busy with kingdom-building business here on earth. We are here to tell someone about the goodness of Jesus and what He has done for us, and to stay in the Word and pray for those who don't know Him. We are to be dressed in our full armor of God (Eph. 6:11 NIV) so we can withstand the attacks of the enemy.

We should remember God will not put a dream or vision in our lives without bringing it to reality. He gives us strength for the journey of life, and thus a strong people have faith that they are strong enough for the journey, but people of strength have faith that it is the journey that will make them strong. "Therefore go and make disciples of all nations" (Matt. 28:19a NKJV). Therefore, where God guides, He always provides, directs, strengthens, and protects because ultimately it is all to His glory.

WHICH WAY TO GO

How do we know which path to take and which way to go? A new career or job relocation, a new relationship, and a residential move, family dynamics changed through separation, divorce, or death—all are lifestyle choices to be made sometime. Our hearts are influenced by the events that occur around us, and our spirits cry out to know God's way, in order to be taught and led into His truth. But we cannot discern the way unless God shows us, we cannot learn the path unless God teaches us, and we cannot walk in truth unless God leads us. Faithfully we should seek understanding of the plans that He delights in prescribing for human conduct, how He bestows favor upon mankind, and the plan by which people are saved.

The idea is apparent that we understand, surrender ourselves to trust in His guidance, and be completely under the direction of God. Moreover, our hope is for eternal life and a lifetime of honesty, faithfulness, and loving kindness that is found in learning which way to go through His Word and a personal relationship with Him. "Show me your ways, O Lord, teach me your paths, lead me in your truth and teach me, for you are the God of my salvation, on you I wait all day long" (Ps. 25:4–5 NKJV). Keep striving to learn which way to go on the path called life.

WHAT'S IN THOSE BAGS?

What's in those bags? Probably it's gifts for a birthday or some other occasion. All the gifts in those bags represent lots of love from the giver to the honoree. As the contents of each bag is received and emptied, pause and think about how many people carry around bags filled with things other than gifts of love. Perhaps their bags contain unforgiveness, anger, sarcasm, worry, shame, brokenness, or doubt. Sometimes we stuff our spouse, our children, our home environment, our jobs, our finances, or our health challenges in bags we carry around with us.

We might change our bags and carry a little bag one time, then a big bag some other time, but we keep the same contents with us all the time wherever we go, in whatever bag that is fashionable with our outfit. Maybe we simply feel comfortable with our bags and our contents. But we don't have to be burdened (or perhaps comforted) with carrying our stuff with us all the time. "For it seemed good to the Holy Spirit, and to us, to lay upon you no greater burden than these necessary things" (Acts 15:28 NKJV). Lay your burdens down in prayer. Begin to sift through the contents and lighten the load of the bags you carry each day. Maybe even throw the bag away once and for all, and that truly might be empowering.

What It Means to Overcome

The act of overcoming means to overpower, to struggle, to get better, to conquer, and perhaps to be victorious! All those definitions have a positive tone, but I'm sure you might still have to participate in some other life changes. Look at some of the things you may have to overcome: is it a prideful, self-centered, me-first attitude, a tight money attitude or a credit card addiction, or an "I'm not going to participate because so-and-so is involved" attitude? Overcome? Why, I am certain you do not have any other traits—like overeating, excessive drinking, smoking, lack of exercise, shopping and hoarding stuff, and social media addiction. Surely there aren't any other hidden habits that you need to adjust or overcome, things that seem to have come over you without much notice or fanfare.

Jesus said, "God is just, He will pay back trouble to those who trouble you and give relief to you who are troubled, and to you as well" (2 Thess. 1:6–7 NKJV). Journal and keep track of situations that need to be addressed as you begin to diligently set aside old ways and habits. Make new plans to overcome some detrimental or unwanted things in your life. Remember that it takes twenty-one days to break a habit and learn a new way of doing, so have a little patience as you strive to overcome and be empowered in your new lifestyle.

WHO IS ON YOUR TEAM?

What does it mean when someone asks, "Who is on your team?" A team is a group of people working together for a coordinated effort or event. Perhaps it could be collecting food to feed the hungry, or serving at a mission or food bank. Maybe your team could provide some homeless folks with enough warm clothes to wear, or blankets to sleep under in winter. Is your team organized to accept donations for an area hard hit with an unexpected catastrophe? Is your team working harmoniously and all on one accord? So much can be accomplished if there is a solid plan of action. Who on your team is giving their time, talent, and treasures without murmuring or complaining?

Overall, a cohesive team should be compassionate, energetic, joyful, and willing to participate. Take note that "I returned, and saw under the sun, that the race is not to the swift, nor the battle to the strong, nor bread to the wise, nor riches to men of understanding, nor favor to men of skill, but time and chance happen to them all" (Eccles. 9:11 NKJV). Seek out and recruit joyful, compassionate, and energetic people who you know will work cohesively on your team. Most of all, your team should not be reproached by the sight, color, culture, or circumstance of the people they volunteered to serve.

WHAT IS HAPPINESS
COMPARED TO JOY?

Happiness comes when we interact with our spouses, children, relatives, friends, coworkers, neighbors, church folks, or strangers on the street. Even though we give short, cordial greetings, we really don't want to exchange too much information; we're happy to simply know them. But joy is to intimately know what is happening in other people's lives so that they can be lifted up in prayer, encouraged, and strengthened during difficult times. The extension of happiness turning into joy will begin when you tell others you value, appreciate, and love them—*and* not for any special occasion or situation.

Joy comes when you share Scriptures and conduct a mini Bible study for greater understanding and witnessing opportunities. It's when you call, write, or visit someone who is sick, or when you cook a meal for a shut-in, run errands, wash clothes, or clean house for a senior citizen. "Go your way, eat the fat, and drink the sweet, and send portions to those for whom nothing is prepared; for this day is holy to our Lord. Do not sorrow, for the joy of the Lord is your strength" (Neh. 8:10 NKJV). The love God has for us is permanently imbedded in us, so set aside some time to let joy in your life overflow to others.

WHOSE SIDE ARE YOU ON?

Sometimes we seem to be easily swayed to choose sides in worldly issues. Recently there have been ongoing controversies and debates regarding the rights, privileges, and number of immigrants allowed into this country. There are certain groups of people who want to limit them. They state that the immigrants are poorly educated, lack nutrition, and have too many medical needs. These immigrant people are accused of putting a strain on the educational system, and they drain off precious resources from existing programs. The critics tend to view them as second-class citizens, and some say they are destitute and don't belong here. Rather than being objective and searching for a concrete equitable solution, we accuse or berate them as the problem.

But we must remember God's grace that was granted to us when we were outnumbered, outsmarted, and unwanted as believers. We do not have the right, power, or authority to pass judgment on another human being's welfare or lifestyle, except in a judicial situation. "Judge not, that you be judged. For with what judgment you judge, you will be judged, and with the measure you use, it will be measured back to you" (Matt. 7:1–2 NKJV). Look for workable lifetime solutions to circumstances instead of judgment against others for the betterment of all.

WHAT'S YOUR GREATEST FEAR?

Fear just what does that mean to you? Is it the loss of your job or income, the loss of your home due to divorce or foreclosure, the unexpected death of your spouse or child, or the loss of mobility due to a debilitating illness or accident? Your greatest fear could be you're not comfortable speaking in front of a group, or you're not able to spell or write or communicate well. Fear could be the loss of your identity or self-respect, the loss of your vision or your purpose in life. It could be a momentary lapse of memory, and all these are real fears.

Sometimes unforgiveness, anger, or bitterness can overwhelm us to the point that life makes it seem like we are going to lose our minds, and then we won't be able to deal with any loss in our lives, and together they culminate into your greatest fear: of not being in control of yourself. But remember "The fear of the Lord is the beginning of knowledge, But fools despise wisdom and instruction" (Prov. 1:7 KJV). Analyze your fears and attempt to deal with when and how they affect you. Minimize your losses by being proactive in and with your life, so that when fear crops up, you will be able to overcome the fiery darts of unwanted situations with a new outlook and a new attitude.

Why You Should Write

Writing prioritizes your daily activities and frees your mind of worry or doubt. If you write, you can have your story survive you, and it's your legacy to let people know about you after you're gone. It's always good to write about the blessings you have graciously encountered, as well as how you survived the missteps of life. Perhaps you'll help somebody to survive and thrive because of your experience. Write your prayers, concerns, and conversations with God in a journal to read later regarding the life experiences that produced pain and sorrow, as well as some growth and wisdom in your life.

Maybe write to a lonely, sick, or shut-in person, someone who can't get out to experience seasonal weather changes, the mountains, or the seashore. Describe it in words for them to visualize in it her mind. Write simply to tell someone you love or miss her. Write about what you have done for others and their response to you. Write to remember the good and work on the bad. Write to take a stand against oppression. Write for no reason at all, except to exercise your brain and the other parts of your body. Keep a pad handy to write down life events, and sometimes write just for the sake of it. "A man's heart plans his way, but the Lord directs his steps" (Prov. 16:9 NKJV).

WHEN IT'S TIME TO MOVE ON

Sometimes you need to move on in life for your own growth, maturity, a new direction, and clarity on some life issues. You need to be able to stand on your own two feet and be self-sufficient and independent. You need to have balance in your life for all of the decisions you make. If where you are is a negative place and is not productive, you need to move on toward the goals you've set for yourself.

Resolve to change something for the better in your lifestyle. If your expectations are too high, then adjust them to a more manageable level. You might need to transition to a place where your light can shine in the darkness to a place of freedom, inner peace, and sanity, and where you can hear God when He speak to you. You certainly need to move on when your joy is gone. It is written, "Better to dwell in a corner of a housetop, Then in a house with a contentious woman" (Prov. 21:9 NKJV). Realize that you don't have to be anxious about moving on as you seek some new or better surroundings that lift, nurture, encourage, and mature you for the purpose that God has intended for just for you. Focus yourself to make a difference and sow seeds for change, for the prosperity of all mankind. Someone is waiting for the light you have to offer, with the direction and guidance you have to share.

WHERE IS YOUR PATH LEADING?

Take a moment and turn away from all the chaos happening in the world. Reflect on the word *path*, which means a trail or track worn down by footsteps; it could be a course or movement taken, as well as a manner of conduct, thought or procedure. Where is your path leading? Did you take a wrong turn and end up in the wilderness of your life? Are you walking on a path of despair, dis-ease, or doubt? Or did you choose a path of righteousness, truth, and integrity? Perhaps you made a decision to unconditionally continue on a path until your life goals are realized. Remember a baby crawls before it walks, training wheels are put on a bike before you learn to ride proficiently, and God's Word will guide you in the way you should go. "I will bring the blind by a way they did not know; I will lead them in paths they have not known. I will make darkness light before them, and crooked places straight. These things I will do for them, and not forsake them" (Isa. 42:16 NKJV).

You will be blessed as you continue down some paths that are familiar, and perhaps you'll venture onto some new paths overflowing with challenges and opportunities of integrity, peace, and the joy of living. After maturing through your missteps, you will be confident to categorically know where your path is leading on the main highway of life.

WHAT WILL YOU DECLARE?

To declare means to reveal, announce openly, make a statement, speak positively and emphatically, or make your opinion known. What you speak has a dimension to make a change, to influence, to encourage, to praise and worship, to preach and teach, to love, to forgive, and to speak life. Believe it or not, your opinion counts, your beliefs matter, and your words have the power to ignite for good. What you declare has great power and merit, and it has the ability to change a situation and impact the surrounding environment by what you say. If you emphatically declare all of the blessings you have experienced in your life, than your attitude and outlook will surely change for the better. "This is the message which we heard of him, and declare unto you, that, God is light and in him is no darkness at all" (1 John 1:5 KJV).

Keep your declarations within eyesight to remind you that you are blessed and not cursed, the head and not the tail, rich and not poor, healthy and not sick or handicapped, happy and not sad, loved and not shunned. You have clothes to wear and are not naked, you have food to eat and are not hungry, you have a place to live and are not homeless, and you have sight and are not blind. Hopefully, you will realize you are able to hold your head up, walk in His marvelous light, and declare His goodness in all that you have experienced. It is guaranteed you will exhibit an uplifting difference within yourself, your home, your workplace, and especially in your prayer life by what you declare.

WORKING FOR YOUR HARVEST

What is the expected result of working for your harvest? Work first started in the Garden of Eden, when all Adam had to do was name the animals and tend the garden. In the beginning, work was designed to be necessary but pleasurable, and it was to have seeds to sow into the kingdom. However, it is written that "If a man will not work, he shall not eat" (2 Thess. 3:10 NIV). In order to receive a harvest, you must first sow some seeds. Only seed sown is harvested, and a supply of seed is given to the sowers of seed. Think about it! There are many different varieties of seeds to be sown and harvested.

Sowing *self-seeds* is learning to sow you into a purpose larger than yourself for the benefit of others. *Tithe-seeds* are giving a tenth of your first fruit offering, whether it's your money, time, creativity, or talent. *Faith-seeds* are your prayers, faith, fellowship with others, and your accomplished commitments. "Give, and it shall be given unto you; a good measure, pressed down, and shaken together and running over, shall men give into your bosom" (Luke 6:38a KJV). In a depressed economy of uncertain job prospects, dwindling wages, home foreclosures, increased food prices, and student loan debt, it is questionable to give if you have little or nothing to give. But consider some new ways to grow your harvest with the work of your hands, head, and heart, which eventually will produce some expected harvest results for today and beyond.

WHAT EMPTY MEANS

Empty means to contain nothing; to be vacant, unoccupied; to have no meaningful purpose or direction; to pour out or remove. Is it a good place to be in, perhaps as a place to be devoid of anger, bitterness, loneliness, pride, envy, and self-loathing? However, empty is also a place to be filled with the love of your spouse, children, coworkers, neighbors, church folks, and others around you. Empty is a good place to get acquainted with your purpose and calling, your spiritual gifting, or your passion in life. Empty is also a place to be filled with a zest for living with energy, good health, presence of mind, and the ability to persevere.

Without doubt, empty is a great place to be filled with knowing that this day belongs to Him. "Therefore do not be unwise, but understand what the will of the Lord is" (Eph. 5:17 NKJV). It is definitely having the ability to withstand the schemes of the devil with prayer and the Word. Empty means to be filled with peace, love, joy, and forgiveness. Consider when you make a list of all the things that should be and must be emptied out of your life to make some room for what the future has in store for you. "Finally brethren, farewell. Be complete, be of good comfort, be of one mind, live in peace; and the God of love and peace will be with you" (2 Cor. 13:11 NKJV).

What Would You Give Up?

What would you give up to be alive and free? Your career? Probably not, because income is needed to pay your bills and living expenses. Would you give up your spouse, children, relatives, or close friends? No, because bonds of love and long-lasting attachments have been formed, and giving them up probably won't work. Would you give up your home? Perhaps not; your home represents a place of refuge, security, peace, and sanctuary of sanity. But think about what you would give up if the circumstances presented themselves.

Well, you could consider giving up pride, bitterness, anger, jealously, envy, insecurity, and unforgiveness. Maybe you can give up the love of money, the worship of other gods, social media, and the things that rule your daily life. That's a lot to give up, but it would be worth it to be alive and free, undo or redo a situation, and initiate a new beginning on a fresh slate in your life. It's worth every effort. "Stand fast therefore in the liberty by which Christ has made us free, and do not be entangled again with a yoke of bondage" (Gal. 5:1 NKJV). Start by developing a habit of reading the Word daily. Journal your prayers and God conversations, and open yourself up to the overflow of the fruit of the Spirit (Gal. 5:22–23). Sing joyous songs of praise, and give your old self away for a new attitude to be used in a way you have never known before.

WHAT IS ENVY?

Envy is having hatred and ill will in your heart and mind; it's a feeling of discontent because of another person's advantages. It is being resentful or jealous, and it also means to covet or long for something or someone that does not belong to you. Envy is a form of denying your uniqueness because we are all fearfully and wonderfully made. Envy divides your attention from kingdom-building business, reading and studying the Word, and maturing in your prayer life. Invariably, it wastes energy and whittles away valuable time from your spouse, children, work, community service, and church activities.

Could it be that your feelings of jealousy, bitterness, and resentment—which are all wrapped in envy—are causing you to not trust God to be your provider and protector? "For where envy and self-seeking exist, confusion and every evil thing are there" (James 3:16 NKJV). Absolutely it is a waste of time, energy, and brain power to compare yourself to another person, *or* to envy others for what they have. Why not focus on being content with what is happening in your life, the blessings you have encountered, and all that God has already done for you? Be obedient to trust in your own life purpose, pattern, and plan. Most of all, be happy and realize you may already have more than you deserve, and probably more than you could ever use. Happiness, not envy, should be your choice.

WHY CHANGE IS GOOD

Change happens in our lives, sometimes for reasons beyond our control or understanding. It is often the act of taking, replacing, converting, or substituting one thing for something else. Change might be a move to another house, another state, or another part of the country; it could be a career change. Perhaps it's going from one school to another. Some marriage situations change due to divorce or death. Maybe an injury or illness will cause an unwarranted change in your life, and you certainly will change as you grow older.

However, change is good if we face it and accept it with obedience and dignity. Change is a chance to be challenged and strengthened, to have the ability to stand on our faith, the promises of God, and His Word. Realize that everything we encounter in life is constantly changing for good, because God is molding, shaping, and maturing us for our kingdom journey. "The Lord is near to all who call upon Him. To all who call upon him in truth. He will fulfill the desire of those who fear him; He also will hear their cry and save them" (Ps. 145:18–19 NKJV). Don't fight against change, use it for good and allow it to make a difference in your life situations, as you sow seeds for change out in the world for eternity.

WHAT'S LOVE ALL ABOUT?

What's love all about? Is it used as a temporary passion that dries up after a while, or is it used as a convenience whenever needed? Worldly love is looking out for number one, always ready to please yourself and not others. Worldly love is classified merely as an emotion to a physical attraction; it really is lust that seeks to follow after personal sensual desires and take whatever it can get from another person. It seems to be apparent why so many marriages end in separation, dysfunction, or divorce. The world's love takes, but God's love gives; it is not self-indulgent, and the very love that is part of His essence is sacrifice. His love kept Jesus hanging on the cross for our sins, sacrificing His life for ours. "Greater love has no one than this, that he lay down his life for his friends" (John 15:13 NIV).

True love involves looking out for the best interests of someone else rather than yourself. Consider what kind of love you exhibit in your everyday life. Will you be known as friendly, kind, honest, and trustworthy? Will you be known as a giving, caring, sharing person? People may know you as an affectionate person, and you are a Christian by the way you act toward others. So what's love all about? It's about making a difference in life by sprinkling some joy and lots of love around in the garden of the world.

Working in the Kingdom

God's original plan intended to extend His heavenly kingdom to earth and bring His invisible supernatural rule into the visible, natural domain. Working in the kingdom is really about returning to the governing authority of God and learning how to function in that authority. It is God's redemptive reign, both individually and collectively through His government established on earth. It has already come to us in the person of Jesus Christ, who was sent to die for our sins, overcome evil, and deliver us from its power.

Our citizenship in the kingdom comes from our acceptance of eternal life through Jesus Christ as our personal savior. Working in the kingdom denotes all areas of physical, mental, spiritual, economic, social, and moral aspects of human life affected by God's reign. The land and all who live on it are affected, as well as life, death, sickness, and disease. However, it is incumbent on all of us to be good stewards over what God has given us and be thankful for the opportunity to be working in the kingdom. "Go into all the world and preach the gospel to every creature" (Mark 16:15 NJV). Go out and give yourself away to be used in the kingdom every day, to make the world a better place for all to prosper.

WHAT ARE YOUR WORDS WORTH?

When you speak, do you stand behind a promise or a vow unto completion? Are you a person of integrity, truth, or openness? Do you build up or tear down with your words, encourage or dishearten? Do you think before you open your mouth to speak? Sometimes it is not what you say but how you say it, whether it is received in the right vein to help, energize, and perhaps motivate someone to action. Do you teach, communicate, and demonstrate positive aspects of a healthy lifestyle by your words or actions? Your words are worth more than money can buy, especially if they are words of forgiveness, love, healing, and prayer. Negative, harsh, angry, and prideful words cannot be reclaimed. Consider and think about the words you speak, and in what tone of voice. Are they words of blessings, gratitude, patience, and kindness? "Soft answer turns away wrath, but grievous word stir up anger" (Prov. 15:1 KJV).

Remember that you alone have the power to speak life into yourself, your spouse, your children, your neighborhood, your workplace, your finances, your health issues, and even into some church situations. Contemplate what your words are worth, and use them wisely to speak life out into the kingdom.

WE'RE ALL TOGETHER

Daylight Savings Time always amazes me. We think we can manipulate time, but it still remains twenty-four hours for one day on the clock. Did we save any daylight? We simply move the clock so we can have an additional hour of sunlight in the warmer months. Most notably, we're all together in the beginning of a life process. All are thinking together in unity and working together to achieve success, no matter the movement of time. We attempt to come to an understanding about what is significant in our lives. Is it the slowed economy, the foreclosed housing market, or rapidly rising gasoline prices? Could it be increased insurance, utilities, food, or clothing prices? What about unaffordable college tuition, scarce employment, and unobtainable career paths?

As discouragement slowly creeps across the land, it makes us realize that no matter where we live, work, or worship, we're all together in the process of life. No one—rich or poor, black or white, resident or immigrant—is separated from life situations that befall us as we continue to strive for the better things in life. David reminds us, "Behold, how good and how pleasant it is for brethren to dwell together in unity" (Ps. 133:1 NKJV). Recognize how blessed you are when you go among the poor, orphans, widows, the homeless, the helpless, and those who have lost hope. Make a difference with a smile, a kind word, maybe a few groceries, or some bus fare. Pay for a haircut or perhaps buy an article of clothing if needed. Most of all, remember that we're all together in this place in space called America.

WALKING

What are the traits of walking and the benefits associated with this movement of the body? It is the rhythmic action of putting one foot in front of the other and moving forward. You don't have to worry about needed equipment, because there is none. Whether in a walking club or on your own, it is great physical activity. Whether your mood is up or down, whether you feel in or out of sorts, and whether you feel you are in the upper realm of your pursuit or on the lower rung, it really doesn't seem to matter—just keep walking! Maybe it will benefit you to keep walking toward your goal of receiving your degree, obtaining financial security, or renewing family dynamics after death, divorce, or illness. Maybe it's walking toward a renewed relationship with a friend or a right relationship with the One who makes everything possible in life.

Find out what your purpose and calling is and keep walking toward your destiny and the completion of your assignment, whatever it may be. "For you have delivered me from death, and my feet from stumbling that I may walk before God in the light of life" (Ps. 56:13 NIV). Be encouraged to keep walking for physical stamina, a long life span, and calmness of mind. Walking is good for the preparation of upcoming events, speeches, or projects. Positively walking affords you a great opportunity to pray, sing praises to God, and get some quiet 'me time'.

YOUR PURPOSE AND CALLING

Do you know what your purpose and calling is for your life? Your primary purpose is to worship God and to tell someone about the goodness of Jesus and what has happened in your life. Throughout history, men and women were called for specific purposes in their lives, and they responded under a plethora of circumstances. They stood up for the underclass against oppression of their civil rights, as well as unjust laws that still keep the rich separate from everyone else. They stood up for poverty, the homeless, and the helpless and forgotten people. They forged ahead to make a difference and sow seeds for change. Their purpose and calling went beyond themselves, and they passionately sought to love, to give, to be a light, and to do what was right for other people.

David wrote, "That I may publish with the voice of thanksgiving, and tell of all thy wondrous works" (Ps. 26:7 KJV). It's not difficult to ascertain what your purpose and calling is. It's whatever you're passionate about or what you continuously do that works well and brings joy to you. As a result of your service to others, continue to joyously walk in your purpose and calling until your fulfillment is accomplished.

YOUR RIGHT TO VOTE

Voting for president comes every four years, and there are some elections every two years for various other offices. We all have important parts to play in the game, and it's your right to vote if you are registered. Congress in 1869 passed the fifteenth amendment and ratified it in 1870. After the Civil War, many Southern states continued to have discriminatory practices, including literacy tests as a prerequisite to vote. The Voting Rights Act of 1965 was signed into law by President Lyndon Johnson as an act to enforce the fifteenth amendment to the constitution of the United States. Many people in the South were harassed and intimated, and they experienced economic hardships, physical violence, and even death for the right to vote.

The Declaration of Independence gave us certain freedoms from the influence and control of others, but those rights and privileges were based on the ideas of men. However, if you do not claim, realize, and exercise your right to vote, it might slowly slip away. Know without question that your right to vote is crucial. "But as for you, brethren, do not grow weary in doing good" (2 Thess. 3:13 NKJV). Exercise your right to vote, and encourage others to vote because it is an honor to be able to vote for the candidates or issues of your choice.

YOUR VOICE

What can you do with your voice? Sing, talk, rejoice, praise, pray, and worship. Soothe and hum to a crying baby with your favorite song. Incite, whisper, scream, and do a lot of other things as well. You might even be able to change an unfavorable situation with a calm voice. You can forgive and heal, lead and instruct. You can teach and uplift with your voice or tear down, love or hate with your voice—it's your choice. It's a good possibility that you can forgive and heal with your voice. Most important, use your voice to advocate for the homeless, the less fortunate, the helpless, and the lost folks.

Use your voice to amend old laws and help pass new ones when and where needed. Stay positive and don't use your voice to murmur and complain, because that's a waste of time, energy, and brain power. There is so much you can do with your voice. Think of all the ways you can positively make a difference and sow seeds for change. "The heavens declare the glory of God, and the firmament shows his handiwork. Day unto day utters speech, and night unto night reveals knowledge. There is no speech nor language where their voice is not heard" (Ps. 19:1–3 NKJV). Your voice can proclaim the goodness of what God has done for you to the ends of the earth and to all who will listen and then rejoice in the glory of His presence.

Words of Encouragement

"Thanks for writing a blessing each Monday morning." —Denise W.

"Great words this week. Thanks." —Mary R.

"A fantastic way to start the week." —Alicia M.

"Your writing on Monday morning is a great encouragement." —Carol H.

"Keep it coming every Monday." —Bethany K.

"Right words for this week." —Susanne W.

"How wonderful to read such great and encouraging words." —Lena P.

"Thank you for writing words of encouragement." —Kevin H.

"Amen, amen, amen, and thanks for writing to us." —Jackie P.

RECOMMENDED READING

Adams, Jay E. *Wrinkled but Not Ruined: Counsel for the Elderly*. Woodruff, SC: Timeless Texts. Copyright 1999.

Cloud, Henry, Dr. *Changes That Heal, How to understand your past to ensure a healthier future,* Zondervan, Grand Rapids, Michigan. Copyright 1992

Heaven Calling: Hearing Your Father's Voice Every Day of the Year— Devotions from Genesis to Revelation. Grand Rapids, MI: Worthy Media, Inc., Copyright 2010.

Mayhall, Carole. *Words That Hurt, Words That Heal*. Colorado Springs: NavPress Books and Bible Studies. Copyright 1986.

McGee, Robert S. *The Search for Significance*. Nashville, Tennessee: W Publishing Group, a Division of Thomas Nelson, Inc. Copyright 2007

Trimm, Cindy. *Commanding Your Morning*. Lake Mary, FL: Charisma House Book Group. Copyright 2007.

Printed in the United States
By Bookmasters